WHEN MEN LEAD WELL

Restoring Strength, Responsibility, and Purpose

by

Lemuel King

WHEN MEN LEAD WELL

When Men Lead Well

Scripture quotations, if used, are taken from the Holy Bible, [version], unless otherwise noted.

First Edition

ISBN: 979-8-9999942-4-0

DEDICATION

To every man who has ever stood at a crossroads and wondered if he had what it takes…

To every man who has carried a silent weight, fought an invisible battle, or pressed forward without applause…

To every man who has led through strength, and also led through brokenness…

To every man who kept going even when quitting felt easier…

This book is dedicated to you.

It is dedicated to the fathers who get up every morning not because they feel strong, but because someone in their home depends on them.

To the husbands who love with patience, protect with wisdom, and fight for their families even when the world pulls at them from every direction.

To the sons who are trying to become the men they needed when they were growing up.

To the mentors who stand in the gap and give guidance to those who lack direction.

To the brothers who encourage, correct, challenge, and uplift—helping each other rise a little higher every day.

It is dedicated to the men who lead without needing a spotlight, who pray without needing to be seen, who sacrifice without expecting recognition.

To the men who are healing while still carrying responsibilities.

To the men who are rebuilding after loss, disappointment, or missed opportunities.

To the men who are learning how to lead well because no one ever showed them how—but they are committed to breaking cycles and building new foundations.

This book is for the man who wants to be better.

The man who wants to live with integrity.

The man who wants his life to mean something beyond himself.

The man who believes that leadership is not about perfection, but about becoming who God created him to be.

May this book remind you that your leadership matters.

Your presence matters.

Your decisions matter.

Your journey matters.

And generations will rise and fall based on the seeds you sow today.

To every man who dares to lead well—

This book is for you.

—Lemuel King

THIS IS YOUR CALL TO ACTION:

Decide today that you will lead well.

Not someday.

Not when conditions feel perfect.

Not when you feel fully prepared.

Today. Right now. This moment.

Stand up.

Step forward.

Lead boldly.

Lead humbly.

Lead intentionally.

Lead well.

The future is watching.

Your family is watching.

Your community is watching.

Heaven is watching.

And you are ready

INTRODUCTION

Leadership is one of the greatest privileges a man can ever be given—and one of the greatest responsibilities he will ever carry. No matter your age, title, or background, someone is watching you. Someone is learning from you. Someone is being shaped by the choices you make every single day. Whether you realize it or not, **you are a leader**, not because of a position you hold, but because of the influence your life carries.

You lead when you speak.

You lead when you stay silent.

You lead when you stand firm.

You lead when you walk away.

You lead through your integrity, your discipline, your faith, your work ethic, and your decisions.

Leadership is happening even on the days you don't feel like leading.

In a world filled with noise, comparison, confusion, pressure, and shifting definitions of masculinity, the role of a man has never been more challenged—or more needed. Families need strong men. Communities need steady men. Churches need grounded, discerning men. The next generation needs visible, present, accountable men. And the world needs examples of leadership that are rooted in character, guided by purpose, and strengthened by faith.

This book exists because of a simple truth:

When men lead well, everything changes.

When a man leads well, peace enters the home.
When a man leads well, stability becomes possible.
When a man leads well, respect rises, trust is restored, and order returns.
When a man leads well, children see a model worth emulating.
When a man leads well, a community becomes safer, wiser, and stronger.

But leadership is not easy—and it was never meant to be.

Every man carries a story.

Every man carries a scar.

Every man carries a lesson learned through hardship or failure.

And every man carries a responsibility he cannot ignore.

This book is not written for perfect men.

It is written for **willing** men.

Men who are ready to grow.

Men who desire to rise.

Men who refuse to repeat cycles that broke generations before them.

Men who understand that their past may explain them, but it does not define them.

Throughout these pages, you will be challenged to step deeper into the leadership God placed inside you. You will confront the places where you've grown comfortable, hesitant, or silent. You will evaluate the strength of your vision, your character, and your daily habits. You will examine the condition of your heart, your relationships, your responsibilities, and your purpose.

Leadership begins with you—before it ever reaches anyone else.

And as you read, you will discover that leading well does not require perfection; it requires **alignment**. Alignment with God's will. Alignment with your values. Alignment with the man you are becoming.

There will be moments in this book where you feel encouraged, and moments where you feel confronted. Both are necessary. Growth requires both grace and truth working together. Leadership demands honesty, discipline, reflection, and courage. Leading well means choosing what is right even when it is inconvenient, unpopular, or misunderstood.

This book is your invitation to rise.

To sharpen your focus.

To strengthen your foundation.

To build what lasts.

To lead in such a way that your presence makes things better, clearer, safer, and stronger.

Your leadership matters more than you know. And as you take this journey chapter by chapter, you will be reminded that your influence is not limited to the people you can see. Generations are impacted by the decisions you make today. Your leadership will reach further than your footsteps ever will.

This is your moment to shift, to elevate, to grow, and to lead with purpose.

Welcome to *When Men Lead Well*—

where leadership is not just a role you play,

but a life you live.

TABLE OF CONTENTS

CHAPTER 1

THE WEIGHT OF LEADERSHIP

There comes a moment in every man's life when he realizes that life is not waiting for him to be ready. Life does not pause until he feels confident. Purpose does not delay until he feels qualified. Responsibility does not shrink until he feels stronger. Leadership arrives long before comfort ever does.

Some men run from this moment.

Some ignore it.

Some deny it.

Some postpone it.

But every man must eventually face it:

There is a weight on your life that cannot be avoided.

You can distract yourself from it.

You can hide behind excuses.

You can busy yourself with noise.

But you cannot escape the truth:

You were created with a calling on your shoulders.

This is the weight of leadership.

And whether you embrace it early or late, willingly or reluctantly, easily or painfully—

the weight remains.

⋆ Leadership Is a Calling, Not a Convenience

Some men believe leadership begins when conditions are perfect—when finances stabilize, emotions settle, relationships strengthen, or opportunities open. But God does not wait on perfect conditions to call a man.

He calls men in their uncertainty.

He calls men in their fear.

He calls men in their brokenness.

He calls men in their struggle.

He calls men in their weakness.

When God called Gideon, Gideon was hiding.

When God called Moses, Moses was stuttering.

When God called David, David was overlooked.

When God called Jeremiah, Jeremiah felt unqualified.

But God said, *"Before I formed thee in the belly I knew thee; and before thou camest forth out of the womb I sanctified thee"* (Jeremiah 1:5 KJV).

Your calling predates your excuses.

Leadership is not something you grow into—

it is something you awaken to.

★ The Weight Is a Signal of Assignment

The weight you feel is not a burden —

it is a signal.

It signals:

- that your presence matters,
- that your decisions matter,
- that your life influences others,
- that your role is greater than you imagined,
- that God placed something on you that cannot be ignored.

The weight is confirmation that God trusted you with responsibility before you trusted yourself.

It is proof that you were built for more than survival.

You were built for stewardship.

The weight is the evidence of your assignment.

★ Leadership Begins in the Invisible Spaces

Leadership does not begin with a microphone, a spotlight, or a platform. Leadership begins in the quiet corners of your life—spaces where no one claps, no one praises, no one notices, and no one sees.

It begins:

- when you choose restraint over retaliation,
- when you choose responsibility over excuses,
- when you choose humility over pride,
- when you choose discipline over distraction,
- when you choose prayer over panic.

These invisible choices build a man's visible leadership.

The Scripture says, *"He that is faithful in that which is least is faithful also in much"* (Luke 16:10 KJV).

What you do when it doesn't seem to matter determines how much God can trust you when it does.

The Weight Forms a Man's Character

Responsibility is one of God's methods for shaping men.

Pressure does not destroy purpose—it develops it.

Under the weight of leadership, a man learns:

- patience,
- discernment,
- emotional control,
- sacrifice,
- courage,
- and spiritual dependence.

Leadership exposes what must be strengthened, healed, corrected, or matured. Not because God is displeased with you, but because God is preparing you.

This is why Scripture says, *"The trying of your faith worketh patience"* (James 1:3 KJV).

Pressure grows the man

that comfort could never produce.

Leadership Requires Knowing Who You Are

A man cannot lead well if he does not know who he is.

And he cannot know who he is until he understands who God says he is.

You are not defined by:

- your mistakes,
- your past,
- your failures,
- your upbringing,
- your insecurities,
- or your fears.

You are defined by the God who formed you.

"I will praise thee; for I am fearfully and wonderfully made" (Psalm 139:14 KJV).

Leadership requires identity.

Identity requires revelation.

Revelation requires relationship.

The more a man grows in God,

the more he grows into himself.

The Weight Doesn't Wait for Perfection

Some men sabotage their leadership waiting to become perfect. They disqualify themselves before God ever does. They assume leadership requires flawlessness, strength at every moment, and answers to every question.

But God never asked for perfection.

He asked for willingness.

Moses doubted his speech.

Gideon doubted his confidence.

Timothy doubted his age.

Jeremiah doubted his strength.

But God said to Paul, *"My strength is made perfect in weakness"* (2 Corinthians 12:9 KJV).

Leadership is not about being flawless—
but about being faithful.

The Weight Demands Accountability

One of the most dangerous traps for men is isolation—
leading alone, suffering alone, thinking alone, falling alone.

Isolation weakens leadership because isolation blinds leadership.

Scripture says, *"Iron sharpeneth iron"* (Proverbs 27:17 KJV).

Sharpening requires friction.

Sharpening requires proximity.

Sharpening requires vulnerability.

A man cannot be sharpened at a distance.

Accountability strengthens a man by:

- challenging blind spots,
- confronting excuses,
- encouraging consistency,
- providing safety during struggle,
- strengthening character,
- and preventing foolish decisions.

Strong men seek sharpening.

Weaker men avoid it.

Leaders embrace it.

The Weight Demands Emotional Strength

Leadership is not simply a mental or physical assignment—it is an emotional and spiritual one.

A man must learn to lead his emotions so his emotions do not lead his decisions.

Scripture teaches, *"He that hath no rule over his own spirit is like a city that is broken down, and without walls"* (Proverbs 25:28 KJV).

A man who is ruled by emotion cannot protect what God gave him.

A man who controls his spirit becomes unshakeable.

Leadership requires emotional discipline—
the ability to:

- stay steady when others panic,
- stay patient when others rush,
- stay calm when others react,
- stay grounded when others lose direction.

Emotional stability is leadership security.

Leadership Is a Gift You Grow Into

No man wakes up fully prepared for the leadership God places on him. Leadership is not immediate—it is progressive. It is not delivered—it is developed.

God grows leaders through:

- responsibility,
- repetition,
- pressure,
- mistakes,
- correction,
- and endurance.

This is why Paul wrote, *"I have fought a good fight, I have finished my course, I have kept the faith"* (2 Timothy 4:7 KJV).

Leadership is a journey—

not an event.

The Weight Will Not Break You

There will be days when leadership feels heavy.

There will be moments when responsibility feels overwhelming.

There will be seasons when you question your strength, your direction, and your ability to lead well.

But hear this clearly:

The weight placed on you was built for the man within you.

God never strengthens a man for a burden he will not carry, and He never places a burden on a man He will not strengthen.

"I can do all things through Christ which strengtheneth me" (Philippians 4:13 KJV).

The weight is not your enemy—
it is your trainer.

The weight is not your downfall—
it is your development.

The weight is not your punishment—
it is your preparation.

This Is the Moment Leadership Begins

Leadership begins the day a man stops running from the weight and starts *rising* beneath it.

You rise when you choose responsibility.
You rise when you embrace assignment.
You rise when you walk in identity.

You rise when you accept accountability.

You rise when you step forward—

even with trembling hands.

A man becomes a leader the moment he decides:

“I will no longer shrink.

I will no longer hide.

I will no longer avoid.

I will rise.”

Because leadership is not about being ready—

it’s about being willing.

This Is Your Call to Rise

The world needs men who are not afraid of the weight.

Homes need men who will step into responsibility.

Generations need men who will model strength.

Communities need men who will walk with conviction.

God is calling for men who will stand, lead, and become who He destined them to be.

You are that man.

This is that moment.

And this is the weight

that will shape the leader

you were born to become.

CHAPTER 2

LEADING YOURSELF FIRST

Every man desires influence. Every man desires respect. Every man desires impact. But God has an order, and no man can bypass that order:

Self-leadership comes before public leadership.

Private discipline comes before public impact.

Inner mastery comes before outer authority.

If a man does not rule himself, nothing he tries to rule will remain stable.

If a man does not lead himself, his leadership of others will eventually collapse.

This is why Scripture says plainly:

"He that ruleth his spirit is better than he that taketh a

city."

— Proverbs 16:32 (KJV)

Conquering yourself is the highest conquest.

Leading yourself is the highest leadership.

★ THE FIRST ARENA OF LEADERSHIP IS THE INNER WORLD

Life will try to teach men that leadership starts with followers, titles, accomplishments, or positions. But real leadership is forged in the unseen areas of a man's inner world.

This is the world of:

- thoughts,
- habits,
- emotions,
- self-discipline,
- spiritual alignment,

- convictions,
- and quiet decisions.

These internal battles shape external results.

A man wins outwardly

after he has conquered inwardly.

Jesus taught this truth when He said,

"Cleanse first that which is within..."

— Matthew 23:26 (KJV)

If the inside is not in order,

the outside can only imitate leadership — never sustain it.

A MAN MUST FACE HIMSELF BEFORE HE CAN LEAD ANYONE ELSE

The hardest person for a man to lead is the person he sees in the mirror.

That man carries:

- his insecurities,
- his frustrations,
- his old wounds,
- his childhood patterns,
- his learned behaviors,
- his hidden fears,
- and his silent battles.

Some men avoid this confrontation for decades.

They lead loudly but live quietly broken.

They project confidence but privately battle chaos.

Self-leadership forces a man to stop running from himself and start wrestling with himself.

This is why Scripture challenges us:

"Examine yourselves..."

— 2 Corinthians 13:5 (KJV)

Self-examination is spiritual surgery.

And no man becomes great without submitting to it.

SELF-AWARENESS IS THE FIRST SIGN OF SELF-LEADERSHIP

A man cannot change what he refuses to acknowledge.

He cannot build what he refuses to see.

He cannot overcome what he pretends is not there.

Self-awareness is not weakness —

it is spiritual courage.

David modeled this courage when he prayed,

"Search me, O God...

and see if there be any wicked way in me."

— Psalm 139:23–24 (KJV)

Great men invite correction.

Weak men avoid it.

Self-awareness leads to:

- clarity,
- maturity,
- humility,
- responsibility,
- deeper wisdom.

And wisdom builds leadership.

SELF-LEADERSHIP MEANS YOU CONTROL YOU

Before a man tries to control outcomes, life events, or other people, he must control himself.

This means he must rule:

- his schedule,
- his impulses,
- his desires,
- his reactions,

- his tongue,
- his appetite,
- his ambition,
- his time.

Leadership collapses when a man is controlled by anything other than his God-given discipline.

Paul understood this when he declared,

"I keep under my body, and bring it into subjection."

— 1 Corinthians 9:27 (KJV)

Self-leadership is self-governance.

A man who does not govern himself

cannot govern anything around him.

THE MOST DANGEROUS MAN IS THE ONE WHO CANNOT LEAD HIMSELF

A man who cannot lead himself:

- becomes unpredictable,
- reacts emotionally,
- blames others,
- repeats cycles,
- loses credibility,
- squanders opportunities,
- ruins relationships,
- exhausts those around him.

His life becomes a cycle of **starts and stops**,

moments and collapses,

bursts of discipline followed by long valleys of inconsistency.

Leadership requires consistency,

and consistency requires self-mastery.

Scripture describes this kind of instability:

"A double minded man is unstable in all his ways."

— James 1:8 (KJV)

A man without self-leadership is spiritually, emotionally, and mentally unstable.

EMOTIONAL DISCIPLINE IS THE CORE OF SELF-LEADERSHIP

A man who leads himself learns to control his emotions — not suppress them, but rule them.

Uncontrolled emotion:

- destroys trust,
- weakens influence,
- fuels regret,
- damages relationships,
- blinds judgment,
- derails leadership.

Again Scripture warns,

"He that hath no rule over his own spirit is like a city that is broken down, and without walls."

— Proverbs 25:28 (KJV)

A man without emotional walls

invites destruction into every part of his life.

But a man who leads himself emotionally:

- stays calm under pressure,
- responds rather than reacts,
- pauses instead of exploding,
- thinks instead of panicking,
- prays instead of spiraling.

His leadership becomes steady.

His presence becomes grounding.

His influence becomes respected.

THOUGHT MANAGEMENT IS SELF-LEADERSHIP

If a man's thoughts are undisciplined,

his life will be undisciplined.

If his thoughts are chaotic,

his decisions will be chaotic.

If his thoughts are defeated,

his leadership will be defeated.

If his thoughts are elevated,

his leadership will rise.

This is why Scripture commands,

"Bring into captivity every thought..."

— 2 Corinthians 10:5 (KJV)

Men who lead themselves guard:

- what they listen to,
- what they meditate on,

- what voices they allow to shape them,
- what environments they remain in,
- what stories they tell themselves,
- what fears they let linger.

Leadership begins in the mind

long before it appears in the actions.

SELF-LEADERSHIP REQUIRES SPIRITUAL ALIGNMENT

No man can lead himself effectively without God's direction.

He may have motivation, but he will lack divine clarity.

He may have goals, but he will lack God's wisdom.

Scripture promises,

"The steps of a good man are ordered by the LORD."

— Psalm 37:23 (KJV)

God orders steps,

but a man must follow the order.

Self-leadership means:

- you pray,
- you pause,
- you seek God,
- you listen,
- you obey,
- you walk in humility.

A man aligned with God

becomes a man aligned with destiny.

A MAN MUST SAY "NO" TO BECOME WHO GOD CALLED HIM TO BE

Growth requires subtraction.

Leadership requires elimination.

Self-mastery requires refusal.

A man must say NO to:

- old patterns
- childish behaviors
- draining relationships
- destructive environments
- time-wasting habits
- emotional triggers
- spiritual stagnation

Scripture affirms this maturing process:

"When I became a man, I put away childish things."

— 1 Corinthians 13:11 (KJV)

Saying "no" is not rejection — it is protection.

No is the shield of your destiny.

No is the boundary of your leadership.

No is the gate to your next level.

A MAN WHO LEADS HIMSELF CREATES ORDER AROUND HIM

When a man leads himself:

- his home becomes calmer,
- his relationships become healthier,
- his decisions become clearer,
- his work becomes more excellent,
- his influence becomes stronger.

Why?

Because order flows from the inside out.

People can sense stability.

People can feel consistency.

People follow a man who first leads himself.

This is why Scripture says,

"Let your light so shine before men..."

— Matthew 5:16 (KJV)

A man's internal leadership becomes visible light.

GOD PROMOTES MEN WHO LEAD THEMSELVES WELL

Before God elevates a man,

He examines how that man leads himself.

Jesus confirmed this kingdom principle:

"Thou hast been faithful over a few things, I will make thee ruler over many."

— Matthew 25:21 (KJV)

Self-leadership is faithfulness in the "few things."

Promotion is God's response to consistent self-governance.

A man who leads himself well becomes a man God can trust.

THE LEADER WITHIN YOU MUST RISE FIRST

Leadership is not first about leading people.

Leadership is first about leading **your potential**,

your mind,

your habits,

your decisions,

your spiritual life,

your character.

Before your influence expands outward,

it must deepen inward.

Because when a man learns to lead himself:

He becomes a man who can lead anything.

A home.

A marriage.

A team.

A ministry.

A business.

A legacy.

A generation.

Everything begins with **the man inside the man**.

THIS IS THE CALL TO RISE INTO SELF-LEADERSHIP

Not tomorrow.

Not "when things settle."

Not "when life gets easier."

Not "once I feel ready."

Self-leadership begins NOW.

You lead yourself when you decide to:

- confront your weaknesses,
- break old patterns,
- build new habits,
- guard your heart,
- control your emotions,
- discipline your actions,
- strengthen your mind,
- align with God's direction.

Because once a man leads himself,

the world around him begins to change.

CHAPTER 3

VISION: SEEING BEYOND THE MOMENT

Vision is the difference between wandering and walking with purpose.

Between existing and becoming.

Between reacting to life and leading it.

A man without vision moves through life like a traveler without a map—

drifting, repeating, guessing, surviving.

But a man with vision moves with certainty.

He may not know every step,

but he knows the direction.

He may face storms,

but he knows the destination.

He may stumble,

but he never stays down—

because vision pulls him back to his feet.

Vision is God's invitation to rise.

It is God's whisper that there is more in you

than what you have experienced so far.

Scripture declares,

"Where there is no vision, the people perish."

— Proverbs 29:18 (KJV)

When a man's vision dies,

his future begins to suffocate.

VISION IS REVELATION, NOT IMAGINATION

Vision is not simply imagining a better life.

Vision is receiving a divine glimpse of the life God

designed for you.

It is God revealing:

- your identity,
- your direction,
- your assignment,
- your purpose,
- your future impact.

Vision is not daydreaming —

vision is God speaking.

Job declared,

"Thou wilt remember that my life is wind..."

— Job 7:7 (KJV)

A man's time is short —

vision teaches him how to use it wisely.

VISION IS THE LANGUAGE OF DESTINY

Every great destiny begins with vision.

Every transformation begins with insight.

Every God-ordained man in Scripture saw something

BEFORE he became something.

Abraham saw the stars — and became the father of nations.

Joseph saw sheaves and stars — and became a ruler.

Moses saw the burning bush — and became a deliverer.

David saw the giant fall — and became a king.

Paul saw the risen Christ — and became a world-changer.

Before greatness is manifested,

it is first revealed in vision.

Vision is the seed of destiny.

VISION IS OFTEN BORN IN DARK PLACES

Many men believe vision comes in moments of success —

but vision is often birthed in pain.

It is in:

- the quiet nights of disappointment,
- the seasons of brokenness,
- the weight of responsibility,
- the silence after betrayal,
- the tears no one sees,
- the confusion of transition,
- the pressure of leadership—

that God shows a man his true future.

David said,

"Thou hast enlarged me when I was in distress."

— Psalm 4:1 (KJV)

God enlarges vision in distressed seasons.

Your darkest moments may be where your clearest vision is born.

VISION SEPARATES YOU FROM SMALL THINKING

When God gives a man vision,

He also gives him separation.

Vision forces you to break away from:

- limiting conversations,
- average mindsets,
- small expectations,
- unproductive routines,
- generational cycles,
- relationships that refuse to grow.

Abraham was told,

"Look from the place where thou art..."

— Genesis 13:14 (KJV)

You cannot walk into big vision while thinking small.

Vision stretches your mind before it stretches your life.

VISION DEMANDS THAT YOU SEE WHAT OTHERS CANNOT

Men with vision always stand out.

They are misunderstood, questioned, criticized, or underestimated.

Why?

Because vision gives you access to a future others have never seen.

You begin speaking about things they cannot comprehend.

You begin preparing for things they believe are impossible.

You begin dreaming on a level that makes average minds uncomfortable.

Noah was mocked.

Joseph was hated.

Nehemiah was opposed.

Paul was doubted.

But vision made them unstoppable.

It is better to be misunderstood with vision

than accepted without one.

VISION IS THE DISCIPLINE OF FOCUS

Vision eliminates noise.

Vision teaches a man what deserves his attention

and what must be ignored.

Nehemiah declared,

"I am doing a great work, so that I cannot come down."

— Nehemiah 6:3 (KJV)

People with no vision always want you to come down.

They want you lowered to the level where life makes sense to them.

Vision gives you permission to ignore distractions and pursue greatness.

VISION CREATES INNER STRENGTH

Life will challenge your resolve.

People will disappoint you.

Seasons will shift.

Plans will change.

Pressure will intensify.

But when a man has vision,
his inner strength refuses to break.

Vision comforts him in chaos.

Vision anchors him in storms.

Vision steadies him in uncertainty.

Paul said,

"None of these things move me."

— Acts 20:24 (KJV)

Vision makes a man unmovable.

VISION IS NOT FAST — IT IS FORGED

Many men abandon vision because it doesn't manifest quickly.

But God develops vision in stages.

Habakkuk reminds us,

"Though it tarry, wait for it; because it will surely come."

— Habakkuk 2:3 (KJV)

Vision is forged in:

- small beginnings,
- unseen progress,
- silent seasons,
- character development,
- obedience,
- endurance,
- consistent faithfulness.

Vision is not microwaved —

it is matured.

VISION DEMANDS THE DEATH OF THE OLD YOU

For a man to embrace God's vision for his life,

the lesser version of himself must die.

Vision requires:

- shedding complacency,

- rejecting excuses,
- confronting fears,
- elevating discipline,
- pursuing growth,
- letting old identities fall away.

Paul declared,

"I die daily."

— 1 Corinthians 15:31 (KJV)

Every day, a man either becomes more like his vision

or more like his excuses.

VISION TEACHES YOU TO LIVE WITH PURPOSE

Vision does not simply show you where you're going—

it shows you how to live today.

It clarifies:

- how you speak,
- how you behave,
- how you plan,
- how you invest your time,
- how you steward your gifts,
- how you pursue excellence,
- how you handle pressure,
- how you love your family.

Vision is not someday —

vision is every day.

VISION MAKES A MAN GENERATIONAL

When a man walks in vision,

his footsteps become a path others can follow.

His children gain direction.

His home gains stability.

His marriage gains strength.

His decisions gain weight.

His name gains honor.

Scripture teaches,

"A good man leaveth an inheritance to his children's children."

— Proverbs 13:22 (KJV)

Vision is inheritance.

Vision is direction.

Vision is legacy.

A man of vision becomes a man of generations.

VISION MUST BE PROTECTED

Everything God shows you must be guarded.

You must protect vision from:

- negativity,
- doubt,
- fear,
- ungodly voices,
- spiritual attack,
- busyness,
- complacency.

Jesus warned,

"Cast not your pearls before swine..."

— Matthew 7:6 (KJV)

Not everyone is capable of respecting what God placed in you.

Guard your vision

like your future depends on it —

because it does.

VISION DEMANDS ACTION

Vision without action is imagination.

Vision without discipline is fantasy.

Vision without movement is a wish.

God gives vision —

but men must work the vision.

James wrote,

"Show me thy faith without thy works, and I will shew thee my faith by my works."

— James 2:18 (KJV)

Vision becomes reality when a man:

- wakes up with purpose,
- moves with intention,
- builds with discipline,
- sacrifices with conviction,

- obeys with trust,
- perseveres with courage.

Vision is not passive —

it is a command.

VISION IS THE SIGN THAT YOU ARE CALLED TO MORE

A man with vision becomes restless with average.

He becomes uncomfortable with stagnation.

He becomes allergic to small thinking.

Vision is God's announcement

that you were created for more than survival.

Vision is Heaven's reminder

that your story is not over.

Vision is God saying,

"I have not shown you everything yet."

THIS IS THE CALL: BECOME A MAN OF VISION

God is calling men back to vision.

Men who see beyond their job.

Men who see beyond the moment.

Men who see beyond their past.

Men who see beyond their pain.

Men who see beyond their circumstances.

Men who see the future God prepared for them.

Because when a man sees what God sees—

everything rises to match it.

His discipline rises.

His faith rises.

His confidence rises.

His standards rise.

His voice rises.

His leadership rises.

His influence rises.

Vision is the catalyst of becoming.

CHAPTER 4

CHARACTER: THE FOUNDATION OF A MAN'S LEADERSHIP

A man's character is the truest measure of his leadership.

It is the part of him that cannot be faked, borrowed, copied, or imitated.

Character is who you are when pressure hits,

when temptation rises,

when conflict appears,

when no one applauds,

when nobody is watching.

Character is the deepest version of manhood.

It is the frame that holds a man together.

It is the shield that protects him.

It is the compass that guides him.

It is the foundation that carries every weight placed on his life.

Scripture sets the standard:

"A good name is rather to be chosen than great riches."

— Proverbs 22:1 (KJV)

A man's character **is** his name.

Your name goes places long before you arrive.

Your character arrives in every room before your voice ever speaks.

CHARACTER IS THE INVISIBLE STRENGTH BEHIND LEADERSHIP

People often applaud talent, charisma, gifting, intelligence, or success.

But those things are temporary.

They rise and fall.

They inflate and deflate.

They impress for a moment but do not endure.

Character endures.

Character is not quick.

Character is not reactive.

Character does not crumble when tested.

Character is:

- the steady hand,
- the quiet strength,
- the internal stability,
- the spiritual maturity,
- the disciplined spirit

  that makes a man's leadership trustworthy.

Gifts may get a man noticed.

Character keeps a man respected.

CHARACTER IS WHO YOU ARE WHEN GOD IS THE ONLY ONE WHO SEES YOU

The most authentic version of a man is not the version he

shows to people—

it is the version he presents before God.

The private you is the true you.

That is why Scripture warns:

"For nothing is secret, that shall not be made manifest."

— Luke 8:17 (KJV)

The world sees your actions —

God sees your motives.

People see your words —

God sees your heart.

People see your performance —

God sees your integrity.

People see your habits —

God sees your hidden battles.

Real character is forged in the quiet places where applause cannot reach.

CHARACTER ISN'T GROWN IN COMFORT — IT IS FORGED IN PRESSURE

A man becomes strong through the heat of testing.

Character is sculpted by:

- adversity,
- responsibility,
- conflict,
- struggle,
- accountability,
- discipline,
- humility,
- perseverance.

Proverbs says,

"The LORD trieth the hearts."

— Proverbs 17:3 (KJV)

God does not test to **break** a man.

God tests to **build** him.

Pressure clarifies motives.

Pressure reveals maturity.

Pressure exposes weaknesses.

Pressure strengthens endurance.

Character is revealed under weight.

CHARACTER IS BUILT THROUGH THE SMALL DECISIONS YOU THINK DON'T MATTER

A man's greatest victories and failures are found in the subtle moments:

- telling the truth when lying would be easier,
- speaking gently when anger feels justified,
- honoring commitments when quitting feels comfortable,
- resisting temptation when no one would ever know,
- apologizing when pride says, “don’t do it,”
- forgiving when your heart feels wounded,
- choosing consistency when emotions fluctuate.

Jesus said,

“He that is faithful in that which is least is faithful also in much.”

— Luke 16:10 (KJV)

Small decisions develop strong character.

Small cracks destroy it.

CHARACTER IS PROVEN BY RESTRAINT, NOT RELEASE

A weak man releases everything he feels.

A strong man restrains what should not be released.

Character is:

- holding your tongue,
- controlling your reactions,
- managing your emotions,
- choosing wisdom over impulse,
- stepping away from conflict,
- refusing to retaliate,
- staying calm when provoked.

Scripture teaches,

"He that is slow to anger is better than the mighty."

— Proverbs 16:32 (KJV)

A man with character is more powerful than a man who can fight.

Power is not how loud you get

— it's how much control you keep.

CHARACTER PROTECTS A MAN FROM HIS OWN POTENTIAL

Your greatest threat is not your enemy —

it is the unrestrained version of yourself.

Men have lost marriages, careers, ministries, finances,

friendships, reputations, and futures

not because they lacked opportunity

but because they lacked character to hold it.

Pride, lust, anger, secrecy, dishonesty, ego, greed —

these are enemies that don't come from outside,

they come from within.

Scripture warns,

"Pride goeth before destruction."

— Proverbs 16:18 (KJV)

Purpose without character becomes self-destruction.

CHARACTER IS THE FOUNDATION OF TRUST

People follow men they trust.

They avoid men they cannot depend on.

Trust is not built by talent —

it is built by consistency.

Trust is not built by force —

it is built by character.

Trust is not built by speeches —

it is built by reliability.

Scripture says,

"It is required ... that a man be found faithful."

— 1 Corinthians 4:2 (KJV)

Faithfulness creates trust.

Trust creates influence.

Influence creates leadership.

CHARACTER IS REVEALED IN HOW YOU TREAT PEOPLE WITH NO POWER TO REPAY YOU

Your character is reflected in how you treat:

- employees,
- waiters,
- your spouse,
- your children,
- strangers,
- the hurting,

- the misunderstood,
- the overlooked.

Jesus taught,

"Inasmuch as ye have done it unto one of the least of these... ye have done it unto me."

— Matthew 25:40 (KJV)

True character honors the dignity in every person.

A man with character lifts others.

A man without character uses others.

CHARACTER REQUIRES ACCOUNTABILITY

A man without accountability becomes reckless.

A man with accountability becomes wise.

Accountability:

- protects your blind spots,

- strengthens your discipline,
- prevents secret downfall,
- deepens maturity,
- sharpens decisions.

Scripture teaches,

"Iron sharpeneth iron."

— Proverbs 27:17 (KJV)

Even the strongest men need sharpening.

Accountability is not weakness —

it is protection.

The man who avoids accountability

avoids growth.

CHARACTER IS THE GUARDRAIL THAT PRESERVES DESTINY

Destiny is powerful,

but destiny without character is dangerous.

Many men are gifted enough to rise

but not grounded enough to stay.

Character:

- protects your name,
- protects your future,
- protects your influence,
- protects your calling,
- protects your spiritual authority.

God never elevates a man beyond what his character can sustain.

CHARACTER IS SPIRITUAL, NOT JUST MORAL

Character is not just about behavior —

it is about spiritual posture.

It is about:

- surrender,
- obedience,
- humility,
- repentance,
- alignment,
- discipline,
- truth.

David prayed,

"Create in me a clean heart, O God..."

— Psalm 51:10 (KJV)

A man of character guards his heart

because he knows leadership flows from it.

CHARACTER MAKES A MAN WISE

Character shapes how a man handles:

- money,
- relationships,
- conflict,
- temptation,
- opportunities,
- adversity.

It guides him through seasons others fail to navigate.

Scripture says,

"The integrity of the upright shall guide them."

— Proverbs 11:3 (KJV)

Integrity prevents foolish decisions

and anchors wise ones.

CHARACTER BUILDS A LEGACY THAT OUTLIVES YOU

Your possessions will be divided.

Your accomplishments will be forgotten.

Your titles will lose meaning.

But your character becomes your legacy.

Your children will imitate your character

long after they forget your words.

Your grandchildren will benefit from your character

long after they forget your name.

A man's true inheritance

is the character he passes down.

CHARACTER IS THE CALL OF EVERY KINGDOM MAN

God is calling men back to:

- holiness,
- integrity,
- responsibility,
- humility,
- faithfulness,
- discipline,
- emotional maturity,
- accountability,
- spiritual strength.

Character is not optional.

Character is required.

God promotes character.

God favors character.

God uses character.

A man's talent may open doors,

but only character keeps him standing inside the room.

THIS IS THE CALL: BUILD THE MAN GOD CAN TRUST

Not the man who performs well publicly.

Not the man who impresses crowds.

Not the man who hides behind talent.

Not the man who speaks well but lives poorly.

God is calling you to build the man:

- who is honest in private,
- who is consistent in character,
- who is trustworthy in pressure,
- who is faithful in small things,
- who stands firm when tested,
- who guards his heart,
- who walks in integrity.

Because when **character is strong**,

everything around you becomes stronger.

When character is weak,

everything you build becomes fragile.

Build the character

that will carry your calling.

CHAPTER 5

DISCIPLINE: THE PATHWAY TO MANHOOD AND MASTERY

Discipline is not just one trait of a strong man —

it is the **framework** of his entire life.

It is the structure of his habits,

the strength of his decisions,

the maturity of his emotions,

the alignment of his spirit,

and the consistency of his steps.

A man cannot rise above the level of his discipline.

A man cannot lead beyond the strength of his discipline.

A man cannot carry what his discipline cannot sustain.

Scripture makes this brutally clear:

"He that hath no rule over his own spirit is like a city that is broken down, and without walls."

— Proverbs 25:28 (KJV)

A man without discipline is unprotected.

A man without discipline is unstable.

A man without discipline is easily conquered.

Discipline is not optional —

it is the mantle of leadership.

1. DISCIPLINE IS THE HIGHWAY TO PURPOSE

Purpose is powerful.

Purpose is divine.

Purpose is sacred.

But purpose is never fulfilled by wishful thinking.

Purpose is fulfilled by disciplined living.

Purpose is not about having passion —

it is about having patterns.

Purpose is not about having desire —

it is about having direction.

Purpose is not about being called —

it is about being committed.

This is why Scripture teaches:

"The thoughts of the diligent tend only to plenteousness."

— Proverbs 21:5 (KJV)

Diligence — another word for discipline —

builds abundance.

The undisciplined man is constantly fighting regret.

The disciplined man is constantly creating progress.

2. DISCIPLINE IS LEARNING TO MASTER YOUR INNER WORLD

Before a man can conquer anything in the world around

him,

he must conquer the world within him.

A man must master:

- his emotions,
- his impulses,
- his appetites,
- his attitudes,
- his reactions,
- his thought life,
- his spiritual focus.

If he cannot lead himself inwardly,

he will fail outwardly.

Paul understood this spiritual war:

"Bringing into captivity every thought..."

— 2 Corinthians 10:5 (KJV)

Discipline is mental captivity —

you take your thoughts hostage

before they take your destiny hostage.

3. DISCIPLINE MAKES YOU DANGEROUS (IN A HOLY WAY)

There is nothing more dangerous than a disciplined man of God.

Because a disciplined man is:

- focused
- consistent
- unmoved by distraction
- unshaken by pressure
- unbroken by adversity

- unstoppable in pursuit

The enemy fears a disciplined man

because discipline cannot be manipulated.

Temptation loses its power against discipline.

Distraction loses its voice against discipline.

Emotion loses its control against discipline.

A disciplined man moves with precision,

with clarity,

with purpose.

He does not waste time.

He does not waste energy.

He does not waste opportunity.

He becomes a spiritual weapon.

4. DISCIPLINE IS THE FOUNDATION OF EMOTIONAL MATURITY

A man who cannot regulate his emotions

cannot lead his household.

A man who cannot manage anger

cannot manage responsibility.

A man who cannot control frustration

cannot control opportunity.

Scripture gives the blueprint:

"He that is slow to anger is better than the mighty."

— Proverbs 16:32 (KJV)

Emotional discipline is greater than physical strength.

Discipline teaches a man:

- to pause before reacting,
- to breathe before speaking,
- to pray before responding,

- to think before deciding.

This is the essence of male maturity.

5. DISCIPLINE IS A SPIRITUAL WEAPON

Many men think discipline is merely natural —

but discipline is **deeply spiritual**.

Jesus lived a life of relentless discipline:

- disciplined prayer,
- disciplined obedience,
- disciplined silence,
- disciplined restraint,
- disciplined devotion to the Father's will.

His discipline empowered His authority.

Your discipline is spiritual warfare.

Why?

Because every act of discipline:

- weakens the flesh,
- strengthens the spirit,
- silences temptation,
- builds endurance,
- increases clarity,
- aligns you with God's voice.

A disciplined man is a threat to darkness.

\

6. DISCIPLINE DEMANDS SACRIFICE, AND SACRIFICE REVEALS MATURITY

Boys avoid sacrifice —

men embrace it.

Discipline requires giving up:

- comfort,
- convenience,
- excuses,
- laziness,
- instant gratification,
- toxic environments,
- unhealthy habits,
- ungodly influences.

Sacrifice is the price of progress.

Paul speaks of this sacrifice when he says:

"I die daily."

— 1 Corinthians 15:31 (KJV)

Something in you must die daily

for discipline to live fully.

7. DISCIPLINE CREATES ORDER, AND ORDER PRODUCES PEACE

When a man lives without discipline,

his life becomes chaotic.

Without discipline:

- finances collapse,
- time is wasted,
- tasks remain undone,
- relationships are strained,
- emotions are unstable,
- life feels overwhelming.

But discipline creates order.

And order produces peace.

Scripture confirms,

"Let all things be done decently and in order."

— 1 Corinthians 14:40 (KJV)

A disciplined man becomes a calm man

because his life operates with intentional structure.

8. DISCIPLINE GIVES YOU ADVANTAGE OVER YOUR FORMER SELF

Your greatest competitor is not another man —

it is your earlier version.

Daily discipline makes you:

- wiser than yesterday,
- stronger than yesterday,
- calmer than yesterday,
- sharper than yesterday,
- more mature than yesterday,
- more focused than yesterday.

A disciplined man is constantly evolving.

Discipline ensures that who you were

is never better than who you are becoming.

9. DISCIPLINE TURNS PAIN INTO POWER

Discipline hurts.

Discipline stretches.

Discipline demands.

But discipline transforms pain into growth.

It teaches you to:

- endure storms,
- persist through fatigue,
- stay committed under pressure,
- hold your standard when tempted to lower it.

This is why Scripture says,

"No chastening for the present seemeth to be joyous...

nevertheless afterward it yieldeth the peaceable fruit of

righteousness."

— Hebrews 12:11 (KJV)

Discipline has a painful present

and a powerful future.

]

10. DISCIPLINE SETS THE STAGE FOR LEGACY

A disciplined father raises stable children.

A disciplined husband builds a stronger marriage.

A disciplined leader inspires consistent teams.

A disciplined believer becomes a spiritual anchor.

Discipline affects everyone connected to you.

Your family feels it.

Your work feels it.

Your future feels it.

Your legacy feels it.

A man who chooses discipline today

creates blessing for generations tomorrow.

]

THIS IS THE CALL: BECOME A MAN OF UNMOVEABLE DISCIPLINE

A man God can trust.

A man his family can trust.

A man his community can trust.

A man his future can trust.

A man who:

- rises early with purpose,
- prays with consistency,
- works with diligence,
- lives with integrity,
- builds with intention,
- leads with conviction,
- resists temptation,

- breaks generational cycles,
- honors God daily,
- grows intentionally,
- finishes what he starts.

A disciplined man becomes

a **pillar**,

a **protector**,

a **builder**,

a **leader**,

a **legacy-maker**,

a **weapon in God's hands**.

Discipline is not about restriction.

It is about resurrection —

the resurrection of the man God designed you to be.

CHAPTER 6

RESPONSIBILITY: THE WEIGHT ONLY REAL MEN CARRY

Responsibility is the proving ground of manhood.

It is the weight that reveals maturity,

the test that reveals strength,

and the standard that reveals whether a man can truly lead.

Leadership does not begin with a title —

it begins with responsibility.

Manhood does not begin with age —

it begins with responsibility.

Respect is not demanded —

it is earned through responsibility.

This is why Scripture declares:

"For unto whomsoever much is given, of him shall be much required."

— Luke 12:48 (KJV)

Responsibility is God's requirement

for every man who wants to walk in purpose,

carry authority,

and be trusted with more.

1. RESPONSIBILITY IS A CALLING, NOT AN OPTION

Every man is born male,

but not every male becomes a man.

Responsibility is the bridge between the two.

God did not call men to run from pressure —

He called men to carry weight.

This is why the earliest assignment ever given to man was responsibility.

Adam was placed in the garden **to work it and to keep it** — responsibility.

Adam was charged to name every living creature — responsibility.

Adam was given Eve to nurture, protect, and lead — responsibility.

Before God gave Adam a wife,

He gave Adam work.

Before God gave Adam companionship,

He gave Adam calling.

Responsibility came before relationship.

2. RESPONSIBILITY IS OWNING WHAT GOD HAS PLACED UNDER YOUR CARE

Responsibility starts with ownership.

Not ownership of possessions —

ownership of **decisions**, **actions**, and **outcomes**.

A responsible man says:

- "This is mine to manage."
- "This is mine to fix."
- "This is mine to improve."
- "This is mine to steward."

Scripture says,

"Moreover it is required in stewards, that a man be found faithful."

— 1 Corinthians 4:2 (KJV)

A man cannot lead what he refuses to own.

A responsible man accepts:

- the weight of his role,
- the reality of his assignment,
- the consequences of his choices.

He does not hide from responsibility —

he embraces it.

3. RESPONSIBILITY MEANS SILENCING THE LANGUAGE OF EXCUSES

Excuses are comfortable.

Excuses are convenient.

Excuses are easy.

Excuses allow a man to feel justified

in staying exactly where he is.

But excuses are the enemy of destiny.

No man rises while making excuses.

No man grows while blaming others.

No man matures while avoiding accountability.

Responsibility begins when excuses end.

When Adam said,

"The woman whom thou gavest to be with me…"

he forfeited responsibility.

When a man blames:

- his upbringing,
- his circumstances,
- his stress,
- his finances,
- his past,
- his environment,
- his emotions,

he forfeits his authority.

Responsibility speaks a different language:

- "I can do better."
- "I should not have done that."
- "I accept my part."
- "I will fix this moving forward."

Ownership is maturity.

4. RESPONSIBILITY SHOWS UP WHEN LIFE GETS HARD

It is easy to carry small responsibilities.

It is easy to lead when things are calm.

It is easy to be steady when life is simple.

But responsibility is tested in:

- pressure,
- adversity,
- conflict,

- struggle,
- confusion,
- storms.

A man's true character is revealed

in how he responds when responsibility gets heavy.

Joshua was called to lead after Moses died —

and the weight was enormous.

But God told him:

"Be strong and of a good courage..."

— Joshua 1:9 (KJV)

Responsibility requires courage

because responsibility requires consistency

in uncomfortable moments.

5. RESPONSIBILITY IS PRESENCE, NOT PERFECTION

A responsible man does not have all the answers.

He is not flawless.

He is not unbreakable.

But he **shows up**.

He is present even when he is unsure.

He is present even when he is tired.

He is present even when life stretches him thin.

Presence is leadership.

Presence is protection.

Presence is stability.

Scripture tells us,

"Quit you like men, be strong."

— 1 Corinthians 16:13 (KJV)

Quit you like men means:

Act like a man of responsibility.

Stand your ground.

Carry your role.

Stay present.

Your presence in your family brings peace.

Your presence in your home brings order.

Your presence in your calling brings clarity.

A man's presence speaks louder than his words.

6. RESPONSIBILITY IS THE BACKBONE OF FAMILY LEADERSHIP

A man cannot be head of a household

if he cannot carry the weight of responsibility.

Responsibility in the home looks like:

- creating financial stability,

- being emotionally available,
- leading spiritually,
- protecting the atmosphere,
- correcting with love,
- modeling integrity,
- honoring commitments,
- prioritizing family,
- communicating clearly,
- loving sacrificially.

A responsible man becomes the anchor of his home.

His family rests because he is reliable.

His children grow because he is consistent.

His wife feels safe because he is stable.

His home flourishes because he carries the weight.

]

7. RESPONSIBILITY REQUIRES MAKING HARD DECISIONS

A man who avoids hard decisions

avoids leadership.

Responsibility requires:

- saying no when others want yes,
- being firm when it is unpopular,
- choosing long-term strength over short-term comfort,
- admitting when you are wrong,
- having difficult conversations,
- standing for truth even when it isolates you.

Leadership demands toughness,

not cruelty —

but clarity.

Scripture says,

"A double minded man is unstable in all his ways."

— James 1:8 (KJV)

Responsibility eliminates double-mindedness.

A responsible man decides with conviction.

8. RESPONSIBILITY MAKES YOU A BUILDER, NOT A BURDEN

A responsible man is not a burden to his family,

his job,

his church,

or his community.

He is a **builder**.

Irresponsible men drain.

Responsible men strengthen.

Irresponsible men avoid.

Responsible men address.

Irresponsible men complain.

Responsible men create solutions.

A responsible man does not wait for things to happen —

he makes things happen.

9. RESPONSIBILITY EXPANDS A MAN'S CAPACITY

Capacity is the mark of a leader.

Some men collapse under small weight.

Others carry tremendous responsibility with grace.

The difference is not personality —

the difference is responsibility.

Every time a man accepts responsibility,

his capacity grows.

Every time he avoids responsibility,

his capacity shrinks.

Jesus taught this clearly:

"Thou hast been faithful over a few things, I will make thee ruler over many."

— Matthew 25:21 (KJV)

Responsibility earns promotion.

Responsibility enlarges influence.

Responsibility deepens maturity.

God gives more

to men who handle well

what they already have.

10. RESPONSIBILITY BUILDS A LEGACY OTHERS WILL REMEMBER

A man will not be remembered for what he owned.

He will be remembered for what he **carried**.

A legacy is built through:

- consistency,
- sacrifice,
- commitment,
- faithfulness,
- love,
- protection,
- generational leadership.

Your children will not remember every gift you gave —

but they will remember the responsibility you lived.

They will remember that you were there.

They will remember how you handled pressure.

They will remember what you overcame.

They will remember what you stood for.

They will remember how you led them.

Responsibility is the inheritance

that impacts generations.

THIS IS THE CALL: CARRY WHAT GOD HAS GIVEN YOU WITH HONOR

Not with fear.

Not with frustration.

Not with resentment.

Not with avoidance.

But with courage.

With humility.

With diligence.

With faith.

With discipline.

With maturity.

With leadership.

A responsible man becomes:

- a protector,
- a provider,
- a pillar,
- a leader,
- a stabilizer,
- a covering,
- a legacy-maker.

Responsibility is the crown of manhood.

It is the proof of maturity.

It is the weight that shapes kings.

When a man carries responsibility well,

he walks in the fullness of who God created him to be.

CHAPTER 7

COURAGE: THE STRENGTH TO STAND WHEN OTHERS SIT

Courage is the force that separates men who make history from men who simply watch it happen.

Courage is the invisible fire inside a man

that pushes him forward when fear tries to pull him backward.

Courage is not the absence of fear —

it is movement in spite of it.

Courage is not a sign of confidence —

it is a sign of conviction.

And courage is not something inherited —

it is something developed.

This is why God's command to men has never changed:

"Be strong and of a good courage..."

— Joshua 1:9 (KJV)

Courage is not optional for a man who leads.

It is required.

1. COURAGE IS THE INTERNAL DECISION TO STAND UP WHEN EVERYTHING IN YOU WANTS TO SIT DOWN

Fear will always present you with three options:

- Freeze
- Flee
- Fold

But courage gives you only one:

Stand.

Courage says:

- "I may be shaking, but I'm still standing."
- "I may be pressured, but I won't retreat."
- "I may be uncertain, but I will not quit."
- "I may be outnumbered, but I am not outmatched."

Courage is a decision, not a sensation.

David felt the tension of fear,

but he still ran **toward** Goliath, not away.

He ran with a declaration:

"The battle is the LORD's."

— 1 Samuel 17:47 (KJV)

Courage chooses obedience even when emotions resist.

\

2. COURAGE IS DOING THE RIGHT THING EVEN WHEN IT COSTS YOU

Men without courage live by convenience.

Men with courage live by conviction.

Courage costs:

- approval,
- popularity,
- comfort,
- stability,
- ease,
- familiarity,
- sometimes relationships.

But courage rewards:

- respect,
- clarity,
- authority,
- self-respect,

- favor,
- spiritual strength,
- legacy.

Shadrach, Meshach, and Abednego refused to bow

even though the furnace was real.

Their response was courage defined:

"We will not serve thy gods."

— Daniel 3:18 (KJV)

Courage is the refusal to bow

to anything beneath God's calling.

3. COURAGE IS THE COMPANION OF FAITH

Fear fights the mind.

Faith fights the fear.

Courage joins the battle.

Fear says, “You can’t.”

Faith says, “With God, you can.”

Courage says, “Let’s go.”

Scripture makes this distinction:

“For God hath not given us the spirit of fear…”

— 2 Timothy 1:7 (KJV)

Fear is not from God.

So if fear is speaking,

it is not heaven’s voice.

Courage is faith in action.

Courage is obedience under pressure.

Courage is trusting God when you cannot trace Him.

A courageous man doesn’t require full clarity —

just God’s direction.

4. COURAGE IS DOING HARD THINGS WHEN OTHERS CHOOSE EASY THINGS

Comfort is the enemy of courage.

Many men choose the easy route —

the comfortable path —

the non-confrontational method.

But a courageous man does hard things on purpose.

Hard things like:

- apologizing,
- forgiving,
- walking away from temptation,
- holding boundaries,
- breaking addictions,
- confronting sin,
- stepping up,
- speaking truth,
- leading by example.

The easy road never leads to greatness.

Jesus told His followers:

"If any man will come after me, let him deny himself..."

— Matthew 16:24 (KJV)

Denying yourself takes courage.

5. COURAGE IS REQUIRED FOR A MAN TO LEAD HIS FAMILY WELL

A courageous man is not a perfect man —

but he is a present man.

His courage stabilizes his home:

- when finances get tight,
- when decisions must be made,
- when children need strength,
- when his wife needs support,
- when spiritual direction is needed.

Fear will always try to paralyze a husband or father.

Courage empowers him to lead anyway.

Courage says:

"I don't have all the answers,

but I am not running."

"I may not know the future,

but I know the God who holds it."

A courageous man becomes the anchor

when storms hit the household.

6. COURAGE IS SPEAKING UP WHEN SILENCE WOULD BE EASIER

Many men stay silent to avoid:

- conflict,
- backlash,
- disappointment,
- discomfort.

But courage speaks when truth must be spoken.

Courage stands up for:

- his marriage,
- his integrity,
- his purpose,
- his convictions,
- his values.

Jesus Himself said,

"Let your communication be, Yea, yea; Nay, nay."

— Matthew 5:37 (KJV)

A courageous man speaks the truth

respectfully,

lovingly,

and firmly.

Silence is not always wisdom —

sometimes it is surrender.

]

7. COURAGE IS RESISTING TEMPTATION WHEN EVERYTHING IN YOU WANTS TO GIVE IN

Temptation is not a sign of weakness —

yielding to it is.

Courage strengthens a man

at the very moment sin tries to weaken him.

Courage refuses to:

- compromise purity,
- sacrifice integrity,
- destroy discipline,
- entertain what God says avoid,
- indulge in what harms the soul.

Joseph had courage when he said:

"How then can I do this great wickedness, and sin against

God?"

— Genesis 39:9 (KJV)

Courage is the shield

that protects destiny.

8. COURAGE IS QUIET STRENGTH IN DAILY DECISIONS

Not every courageous act is dramatic.

Many acts of courage are silent, unseen,

lived out in ordinary moments.

Quiet courage is:

- choosing patience,
- choosing gentleness,
- choosing humility,
- choosing discipline,
- choosing spiritual growth,
- choosing forgiveness,

- choosing emotional maturity.

Jesus said,

"Blessed are the meek..."

— Matthew 5:5 (KJV)

Meekness is strength under control —

the quietest form of courage.

9. COURAGE PROTECTS A MAN'S MORAL COMPASS

Without courage, a man will:

- drift,
- compromise,
- follow the crowd,
- justify wrong decisions,
- lower his standards.

But courage keeps a man aligned.

Courage holds a man to:

- God's Word,
- God's standards,
- God's purpose.

Psalm 31:24 says,

"Be of good courage, and he shall strengthen your heart."

Courage strengthens conviction.

Conviction strengthens leadership.

10. COURAGE IS THE BIRTHPLACE OF LEGACY

Men are remembered not for the moments they feared but for the moments they stood.

Legacy is built on courage:

- the courage to change,
- the courage to grow,

- the courage to lead,
- the courage to remain faithful,
- the courage to protect family,
- the courage to honor God.

A man of courage may tremble —

but he stands.

A man of courage may cry —

but he moves forward.

A man of courage may feel alone —

but he refuses to bow.

Your children will remember your courage

more than your comfort.

THIS IS THE CALL: RISE IN COURAGE AND LEAD BOLDLY

Courage is not for perfect men —

it is for willing men.

Men who say:

- “Lord, use me.”
- “Lord, strengthen me.”
- “Lord, I will not run.”
- “Lord, I will trust You.”
- “Lord, I will stand.”

God doesn’t need flawless men —

He needs courageous men.

He needs men who will fight spiritually,

love sacrificially,

lead boldly,

pray consistently,

and live obediently.

Because when a man leads with courage:

- he becomes a covering,
- he becomes an example,
- he becomes a pillar,
- he becomes a protector,
- he becomes a legacy-maker,
- he becomes a threat to darkness.

Courage is where leadership becomes conviction and conviction becomes impact.

CHAPTER 8

HUMILITY: THE STRENGTH THAT KEEPS A MAN GROUNDED

Humility is not a soft trait.

It is not fragility.

It is not silence.

It is not weakness.

Humility is strength under full control.

Humility is power that refuses arrogance.

Humility is greatness without boasting.

Humility is confidence without pride.

Humility is authority without intimidation.

Humility is a man knowing:

- who he is,
- who he is not,

- and Who he belongs to.

Scripture is clear:

"Humble yourselves therefore under the mighty hand of God, that he may exalt you in due time."

— 1 Peter 5:6 (KJV)

God does not elevate proud men.

He elevates humble ones.

You cannot rise well if you cannot kneel well.

1. HUMILITY IS THE ANCHOR THAT KEEPS A MAN ROOTED

Every man will experience moments where:

- success tries to inflate him,
- pride tries to creep in,
- accomplishment tries to distort him,
- people try to praise him excessively.

Without humility, success becomes a trap.

Without humility, gifts become idols.

Without humility, blessings become reasons to boast.

Humility is the anchor that keeps a man grounded

when life begins to elevate him.

Jesus said,

"Whosoever exalteth himself shall be abased; and he that humbleth himself shall be exalted."

— Luke 14:11 (KJV)

Elevation without humility leads to humiliation.

Elevation with humility leads to longevity.

2. HUMILITY IS SELF-AWARENESS THROUGH GOD'S EYES

Humility is not thinking less of yourself

— it is thinking of yourself accurately.

Humility says:

"I am valuable, but I am not above correction."

"I am gifted, but I am not self-made."

"I am strong, but I am still dependent on God."

"I am capable, but I still need wisdom."

"I can lead, but I am not the center of the world."

Romans 12:3 teaches,

"Not to think of himself more highly than he ought to think."

Humility is sober thinking.

Pride is inflated thinking.

Humility keeps identity clear.

Pride distorts identity.

A man with humility is balanced.

A man with pride lives off balance.

3. HUMILITY IS BEING TEACHABLE

A proud man stops growing the moment he believes he knows everything.

He stops listening.

He stops learning.

He stops receiving correction.

He stops examining himself.

But humility keeps a man:

- teachable,
- open,
- receptive,
- flexible,
- moldable.

Proverbs 11:2 says,

"With the lowly is wisdom."

Wise men stay low

because that is where God teaches best.

A teachable man becomes unstoppable.

An unteachable man becomes unfixable.

4. HUMILITY IS THE COURAGE TO APOLOGIZE

Pride says:

“I did nothing wrong.”

“I’m not apologizing.”

“I won’t admit that.”

“I’m not humbling myself.”

Pride protects the ego.

Humility protects the relationship.

A humble man apologizes:

- quickly,
- sincerely,
- fully.

He does not blame-shift.

He does not minimize.

He does not justify.

He takes ownership.

James 5:16 commands,

"Confess your faults one to another…"

A man who refuses to apologize

is a man ruled by ego, not purpose.

Humility restores trust.

Pride destroys it.

5. HUMILITY IS PUTTING OTHERS BEFORE YOURSELF WITHOUT LOSING YOURSELF

Humility is not self-erasure.

It is selflessness.

Humility chooses:

- service over status,
- people over ego,
- honor over recognition,
- contribution over competition.

Jesus said,

"The greatest among you shall be your servant."

— Matthew 23:11 (KJV)

If servanthood was the posture of the Son of God,

then servanthood must be the posture of men who follow Him.

A humble man doesn't seek the spotlight —

he seeks to serve.

And because he serves,

God gives him influence.

6. HUMILITY SHIFTS THE ATMOSPHERE OF A HOME

A proud man creates tension.

A humble man creates peace.

Humility in the home looks like:

- speaking gently,
- listening fully,
- apologizing sincerely,
- forgiving quickly,
- being patient,
- admitting mistakes,
- communicating respectfully.

Ephesians 4:2 teaches,

"With all lowliness and meekness, with longsuffering, forbearing one another in love."

Humility builds relationships.

Pride breaks them.

A humble husband brings calmness.

A proud husband brings chaos.

A humble father models growth.

A proud father models stubbornness.

Humility wins hearts.

Pride wounds them.

7. HUMILITY GIVES A MAN SPIRITUAL AUTHORITY

Spiritual authority does not come from:

- shouting,
- demanding,
- controlling,
- intimidating.

Spiritual authority comes from surrender.

A man cannot lead spiritually

until he first kneels spiritually.

Psalm 25:9 declares,

"The meek will he guide..."

God guides humble men.

God strengthens humble men.

God lifts humble men.

Proud men may lead loudly.

Humble men lead powerfully.

8. HUMILITY PROTECTS A MAN FROM HIS OWN EGO

A man's greatest enemy is not Satan —

it is self.

Ego destroys:

- marriages,
- prayer lives,
- careers,
- ministries,
- friendships,
- reputations.

Ego blinds.

Ego isolates.

Ego inflates.

Ego deceives.

Proverbs 16:18 warns,

"Pride goeth before destruction."

Destroy pride

before pride destroys you.

Humility is the safeguard.

Pride is the trap.

9. HUMILITY MAKES A MAN STEADY, NOT FRAGILE

Proud men are easily offended.

Humble men are steady.

Proud men react quickly.

Humble men respond wisely.

Proud men fall apart under pressure.

Humble men stay grounded.

Proud men demand honor.

Humble men earn honor.

Humility strengthens a man's emotional life.

It gives him the ability to:

- absorb criticism,
- process conflict,
- listen carefully,
- grow consistently.

Humility makes a man mature.

Pride makes a man childish.

10. HUMILITY IS THE SECRET TO LASTING LEADERSHIP

Many men rise.

Few men stay risen.

Humility keeps a man from:

- self-sabotage,
- arrogance,
- inflated thinking,

- reckless decision-making,
- moral collapse.

Moses led millions

yet remained meek.

David rose to kingship

yet stayed repentant.

Jesus washed feet

yet held all authority.

Their leadership was not weakened by humility —

it was strengthened by it.

A humble leader lasts.

A proud leader collapses.

11. HUMILITY IS THE GATEWAY TO BLESSING

Every blessing God releases

comes through humility.

God says:

"I dwell... with him that is of a contrite and humble spirit."

— Isaiah 57:15 (KJV)

God draws near to humble men.

God lifts humble men.

God teaches humble men.

God favors humble men.

Every man wants blessing —

but only humble men qualify.

12. HUMILITY BUILDS A LEGACY OF HONOR

A man is not remembered for how loudly he lived

but for how humbly he walked.

Humility impacts:

- your children's memories,
- your marriage's stability,
- your relationships' strength,
- your leadership's influence,
- your community's respect,
- your legacy's longevity.

A proud man may leave accomplishments behind.

A humble man leaves admiration behind.

THIS IS THE CALL: WALK LOW SO GOD CAN TAKE YOU HIGH

If you want God's hand on your life,

stay humble.

If you want influence,

stay humble.

If you want wisdom,

stay humble.

If you want longevity,

stay humble.

If you want peace,

stay humble.

If you want to be a great man,

be a humble man.

Humility is not the loss of strength —

it is the release of true strength.

Because when a man leads with humility:

- God elevates him,
- people trust him,
- family follows him,
- communities respect him,
- legacy remembers him.

Humility is the strength that keeps a man grounded

so God can raise him higher.

CHAPTER 9

INTEGRITY: THE STANDARD THAT SETS A MAN APART

Integrity is the backbone of manhood.

It is the moral strength of leadership.

It is the foundation of trust.

It is the anchor of influence.

It is the proof of character.

A man without integrity may be talented, charismatic,

respected, and admired —

but he will never be trusted.

And a man who cannot be trusted

can never lead well.

Scripture declares:

"The integrity of the upright shall guide them."

— Proverbs 11:3 (KJV)

Integrity is not optional for a man who desires to lead his home,

his community,

his ministry,

or his destiny.

Integrity is the compass that keeps him pointed toward God when temptation tries to pull him off course.

1. INTEGRITY IS ALIGNMENT BETWEEN YOUR PRIVATE LIFE AND PUBLIC LIFE

Some men live two lives:

- the one others see,
- and the one God sees.

Integrity is the commitment to live **one life**.

Integrity is not perfection —

it is alignment.

A man with integrity strives to:

- think what he speaks,
- do what he promises,
- live what he believes,
- practice what he preaches.

Hypocrisy breaks trust.

Integrity builds it.

Jesus condemned double-living when He said,

"Ye are like unto whited sepulchres... outwardly appear righteous... but within are full of dead men's bones."

— Matthew 23:27 (KJV)

Integrity is the refusal to appear clean

while living dirty.

Integrity chooses authenticity

over performing.

2. INTEGRITY IS DOING WHAT IS RIGHT WHEN WRONG IS REWARDED

We live in a world where compromise brings quick gain:

- dishonesty increases profits,
- shortcuts bring applause,
- manipulation brings influence,
- lies bring convenience.

But integrity refuses immediate gain

if it violates eternal values.

Joseph rejected sin because he understood the cost:

"How then can I do this great wickedness, and sin against God?"

— Genesis 39:9 (KJV)

Integrity fears displeasing God

more than losing opportunity.

Integrity chooses the narrow way

even when the wide way looks easier.

Integrity is costly in the moment

but priceless in the long run.

3. INTEGRITY IS WHO YOU ARE WHEN NOBODY IS WATCHING

Public approval means nothing

if a man is privately compromised.

Integrity is:

- the websites you do not visit,
- the conversations you do not entertain,
- the doors you refuse to open,
- the temptations you reject in silence,

- the honesty you maintain when no one can verify it,
- the self-discipline you practice when no one checks.

Psalm 101:2 says,

"I will walk within my house with a perfect heart."

Integrity begins in the home.

Integrity begins in the private place.

Integrity begins in unseen moments.

A man's private life is the truth of who he is.

4. INTEGRITY IS KEEPING YOUR WORD — EVEN WHEN IT HURTS

Your word is the echo of your character.

Psalm 15 describes the righteous man as one who:

"sweareth to his own hurt, and changeth not."

— Psalm 15:4 (KJV)

Meaning:

He keeps his word

even when keeping it is inconvenient, uncomfortable, or costly.

Men without integrity:

- make excuses,
- cancel commitments,
- shift responsibility,
- break promises,
- rewrite truth.

Men of integrity:

- follow through,
- finish strong,
- stay reliable,
- stay consistent,
- honor their vows.

A man's word should mean something.

The moment it stops meaning something,

his leadership loses weight.

5. INTEGRITY IS SPEAKING THE TRUTH — WITHOUT TWISTING IT

Lies have destroyed more men than failure.

Deception erodes:

- trust,
- credibility,
- respect,
- relationships,
- spiritual authority.

Jesus said,

"Let your communication be, Yea, yea; Nay, nay."

— Matthew 5:37 (KJV)

Integrity does not twist truth

to protect image.

Integrity does not omit truth

to manipulate outcomes.

Integrity does not exaggerate truth

to inflate ego.

Truth brings freedom:

"Ye shall know the truth, and the truth shall make you free."

— John 8:32 (KJV)

A man cannot live free

while speaking falsehood.

=

6. INTEGRITY IS MASTERING PRIVATE DISCIPLINE

A man who is undisciplined privately

will be unstable publicly.

Private compromise becomes public collapse.

This is why David prayed:

"Let integrity and uprightness preserve me."

— Psalm 25:21 (KJV)

Integrity preserves:

- your anointing,
- your leadership,
- your spiritual authority,
- your family's trust,
- your destiny's longevity.

Your secret life determines

your public effectiveness.

Do not sabotage your future

with private rebellion.

7. INTEGRITY REQUIRES HUMILITY AND ACCOUNTABILITY

Proud men hide weakness.

Humble men confront it.

A man without accountability becomes:

- self-deceived,
- reckless,
- inconsistent,
- spiritually blind.

But a man with accountability:

- stays grounded,
- stays honest,
- stays teachable,
- stays sharp.

Proverbs 27:17 says,

"Iron sharpeneth iron."

Accountability sharpens integrity.

Secrecy dulls it.

A man who hides his habits

will eventually be destroyed by them.

But a man who submits to wise counsel

becomes a fortress of strength.

8. INTEGRITY IS LIVING WITH CONSISTENCY, NOT CONVENIENCE

Integrity does not change based on:

- mood,
- pressure,
- audience,
- opportunity,

- temptation.

Integrity is consistent.

A man with integrity:

- behaves the same in every room,
- tells the truth in every situation,
- remains faithful in every season,
- keeps the same standards everywhere he goes.

Proverbs 20:7 says,

"The just man walketh in his integrity."

Walketh — meaning continually, repeatedly, habitually.

Integrity is a lifestyle.

9. INTEGRITY MAKES A MAN RESPECTABLE

Respect cannot be demanded.

Respect must be earned.

Integrity earns it.

Men of integrity gain:

- trust from their households,
- honor from their communities,
- credibility in leadership,
- strength in influence.

You cannot buy respect.

You cannot fake it.

You cannot negotiate it.

Respect is the fruit of long-term integrity.

]

10. INTEGRITY IS THE FOUNDATION OF LEGACY

A man will be remembered for:

- how he lived,
- how he spoke,
- how he treated others,
- how he kept his word,
- how he walked with God.

A man without integrity leaves:

- confusion,
- regret,
- broken trust,
- damaged relationships,
- unanswered questions.

A man with integrity leaves:

- honor,
- admiration,

- wisdom,
- consistency,
- a name worth carrying forward.

Proverbs 10:9 declares,

"He that walketh uprightly walketh surely."

Integrity leads a man in a way

that generations can safely follow.

THIS IS THE CALL: BE A MAN WHOSE INTEGRITY CANNOT BE BOUGHT OR BROKEN

A man who:

- stands firm,
- speaks truth,
- honors commitments,
- lives clean,

- rejects compromise,
- embraces honesty,
- protects his witness,
- values his reputation,
- fears God,
- walks uprightly.

Integrity is not the easy path —

it is the right path.

It is the path where God walks with you,

favor follows you,

and legacy flows through you.

Because when a man leads with integrity:

- God trusts him with more,
- people follow him with confidence,
- his family rests under his leadership,
- opportunities open naturally,
- blessings attach to his name,

- and the enemy cannot discredit his witness.

Integrity is not just a virtue —

it is a calling.

It is a standard.

It is a mantle.

And it is the mark of a true man.

CHAPTER 10

DISCIPLINE: THE HABIT THAT BUILDS GREAT MEN

Discipline is the quiet force behind every great man.

It is the internal infrastructure that strengthens a man to

walk in purpose,

lead with authority,

love with consistency,

and stand when others fall.

Talent creates opportunity,

but discipline sustains opportunity.

Gifts will open doors,

but discipline will keep you in the room.

Anointing is powerful,

but without discipline,

anointing becomes mismanaged.

This is why Paul said,

"I keep under my body, and bring it into subjection."

— 1 Corinthians 9:27 (KJV)

Discipline is self-mastery.

A man who masters himself

is a man who can master his environment.

1. DISCIPLINE IS THE DIFFERENCE BETWEEN DESIRE AND DESTINY

Every man desires greatness,

but desire alone does not produce destiny.

Desire is emotional.

Discipline is foundational.

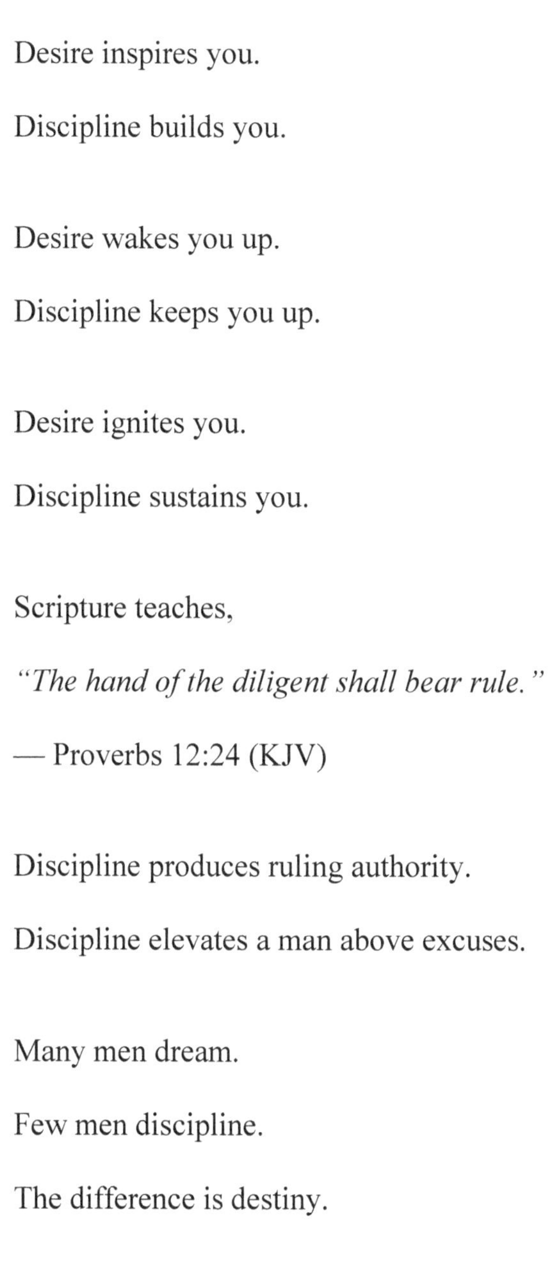

Desire inspires you.

Discipline builds you.

Desire wakes you up.

Discipline keeps you up.

Desire ignites you.

Discipline sustains you.

Scripture teaches,

"The hand of the diligent shall bear rule."

— Proverbs 12:24 (KJV)

Discipline produces ruling authority.

Discipline elevates a man above excuses.

Many men dream.

Few men discipline.

The difference is destiny.

2. DISCIPLINE IS DOING WHAT IS NECESSARY, NOT WHAT IS EASY

The undisciplined man makes decisions based on convenience.

The disciplined man makes decisions based on calling.

Convenience is easy.

Calling takes effort.

Convenience feels good.

Calling demands sacrifice.

Convenience builds excuses.

Calling builds men.

Jesus said,

"If any man will come after me, let him deny himself..."

— Matthew 16:24 (KJV)

Denying yourself is the birth of discipline.

The greatest version of you

is on the other side of what your flesh resists.

3. DISCIPLINE IS CONSISTENCY EVEN WHEN MOTIVATION DIES

Motivation is a spark.

Discipline is the flame.

Motivation is emotional.

Discipline is structural.

Motivation starts you.

Discipline finishes you.

Most men wait to "feel it."

Disciplined men act even when they don't.

"Be steadfast, unmovable..."

— 1 Corinthians 15:58 (KJV)

A stable man produces stable results.

Disciplined consistency builds credibility.

If you cannot be consistent,

you cannot be effective.

4. DISCIPLINE IS MASTERING SMALL DAILY HABITS THAT SHAPE BIG FUTURES

Most men look for dramatic change.

Disciplined men look for daily change.

Small habits become:

- strong mindsets,
- strong routines,
- strong leadership,
- strong spiritual lives.

Jesus taught,

"He that is faithful in that which is least..."

— Luke 16:10 (KJV)

If you cannot master little things,

you cannot manage greater things.

Every area of your future

is hidden in your daily habits.

5. DISCIPLINE IS CONTROLLING YOUR APPETITES BEFORE THEY CONTROL YOU

Every man battles appetites:

- appetite for pleasure,
- appetite for gratification,
- appetite for attention,
- appetite for ease,

- appetite for indulgence.

Discipline is the power to say **no**

to the things that threaten your future.

Paul said,

"All things are lawful unto me, but all things are not expedient."

— 1 Corinthians 6:12 (KJV)

Discipline does not ask,

"Is it allowed?"

It asks,

"Is it beneficial to my destiny?"

A man who cannot control his flesh

will eventually lose his influence.

---

6. DISCIPLINE IS THE FENCE THAT PROTECTs A MAN FROM SELF-DESTRUCTION

Most men are not destroyed by outside enemies.

They are destroyed by:

- unchecked urges,
- unplanned decisions,
- undisciplined habits,
- unmanaged emotions.

Scripture warns,

"He that hath no rule over his own spirit is like a city broken down, without walls."

— Proverbs 25:28 (KJV)

Without discipline,

a man becomes vulnerable to:

- temptation,
- deception,

- inconsistency,
- spiritual attack.

Discipline builds spiritual walls.

7. DISCIPLINE TRANSFORMS EMOTIONAL REACTIVITY INTO EMOTIONAL MATURITY

A disciplined man:

- responds instead of reacts,
- thinks before speaking,
- processes before acting,
- reasons before responding.

An undisciplined man:

- snaps,
- escalates,
- acts impulsively,

- regrets frequently.

Proverbs 16:32 teaches,

"He that ruleth his spirit is better than he that taketh a city."

A man who conquers himself becomes unconquerable.

8. DISCIPLINE ESTABLISHES STRUCTURE SO IMPULSE CAN NO LONGER LEAD YOUR LIFE

Impulse is the enemy of progress.

Impulse:

- spends recklessly,
- speaks harshly,
- reacts emotionally,

- chooses poorly,
- pursues pleasure over purpose.

Structure keeps a man on track.

Disciplined structure looks like:

- prayer routines,
- study schedules,
- financial plans,
- fitness habits,
- boundaries,
- sleep discipline,
- time management.

Structure doesn’t restrict a man —

it focuses him.

9. DISCIPLINE PREPARES A MAN TO LEAD A FAMILY WELL

A man who leads a home must demonstrate discipline in every area:

- self-control in conflict,
- clarity in decisions,
- consistency in behavior,
- stewardship in finances,
- devotion in spiritual matters,
- patience in communication.

A disciplined man becomes a stable man.

A stable man becomes a safe place.

Your family cannot trust what you will not discipline.

Your wife cannot rest in what you will not control.

Your children cannot follow what you will not demonstrate.

Your discipline becomes their security.

10. DISCIPLINE IS THE FOUNDATION OF SPIRITUAL STRENGTH

Spiritual growth does not happen accidentally.

It happens through sacred discipline.

Prayer requires discipline.

Fasting requires discipline.

Repentance requires discipline.

Obedience requires discipline.

Worship requires discipline.

Paul said,

"Exercise thyself rather unto godliness."

— 1 Timothy 4:7 (KJV)

Godliness requires exercise —

spiritual discipline.

A man's spiritual life collapses

when his discipline collapses.

11. DISCIPLINE PRODUCES BLESSING, FAVOR, AND OPEN DOORS

God rewards disciplined men.

Why?

Because He can trust them.

Sow discipline — reap blessing.

Sow consistency — reap credibility.

Sow obedience — reap favor.

Galatians 6:7 reminds us,

"Whatsoever a man soweth, that shall he also reap."

Discipline is the seed

for every future reward.

12. DISCIPLINE BUILDS A LEGACY OF RESPECT

Men are not admired because they want greatness.

They are admired because they **worked** for it.

A disciplined man:

- earns honor,
- builds reputation,
- creates stability,
- inspires trust,
- sets standards,
- changes generations.

Your children will remember:

- your discipline more than your speeches,
- your habits more than your advice,
- your consistency more than your declarations.

Discipline becomes inheritance.

THIS IS THE CALL: MASTER YOURSELF SO GOD CAN TRUST YOU WITH MORE

A disciplined man is unstoppable.

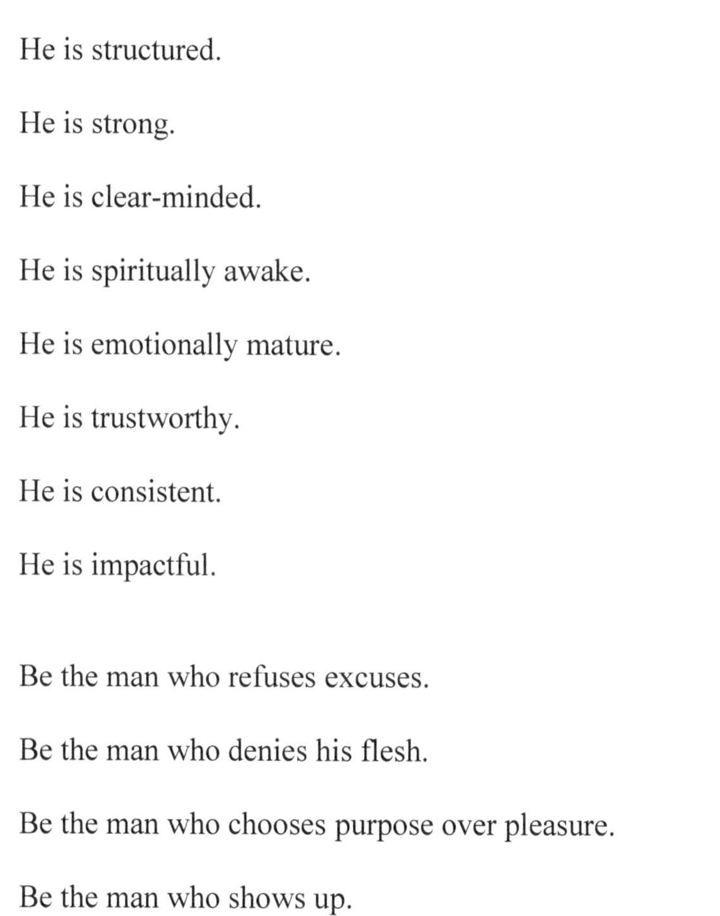

He is focused.

He is structured.

He is strong.

He is clear-minded.

He is spiritually awake.

He is emotionally mature.

He is trustworthy.

He is consistent.

He is impactful.

Be the man who refuses excuses.

Be the man who denies his flesh.

Be the man who chooses purpose over pleasure.

Be the man who shows up.

Be the man who follows through.

Be the man who disciplines himself

so God does not have to discipline him.

Because when a man becomes disciplined:

- destiny becomes reachable,
- purpose becomes attainable,
- leadership becomes natural,
- influence becomes expanding,
- respect becomes lasting,
- and God places more in his hands.

Discipline does not imprison a man —

it frees him to become who he was created to be.

CHAPTER 11

THE POWER OF DECISIONS: CHOICES THAT SHAPE A MAN'S FUTURE

A man's life is a reflection of the decisions he makes daily.

Decisions determine direction.

Direction determines destiny.

Many men blame circumstances.

Many blame childhood.

Many blame environment.

But a man's next level is always unlocked by decisions — not excuses.

God told Israel,

"I have set before you life and death… therefore choose

life."

— Deuteronomy 30:19 (KJV)

Even God will not force a man to decide.

He will present options, guidance, and wisdom —

but the choice belongs to the man.

A man's greatness begins at the moment he decides to be great.

1. DECISIONS CREATE THE PATH A MAN WALKS ON

Life does not move a man —

his decisions do.

A man can pray for direction,

but direction requires decisions.

A man can desire clarity,

but clarity requires commitment.

Scripture warns,

"A double minded man is unstable in all his ways."

— James 1:8 (KJV)

A man who cannot decide

is a man who cannot advance.

Indecision is spiritual paralysis.

Indecision is emotional hesitation.

Indecision is leadership weakness.

A man becomes stable

when his decisions become firm.

2. DECISION-MAKING IS THE FIRST TEST OF LEADERSHIP

You are not a leader because you are admired.

You are a leader because you make decisions.

Leadership lives or dies in decisions:

- The decision to grow.
- The decision to stay disciplined.
- The decision to confront issues.
- The decision to communicate.
- The decision to take responsibility.
- The decision to lead spiritually.

Joshua stood as a leader because of one decision:

"...as for me and my house, we will serve the LORD."

— Joshua 24:15 (KJV)

Strong leadership begins with strong decisions.

3. DECISIONS REVEAL YOUR TRUE PRIORITIES

A man's decisions tell the truth

about what matters to him.

If you want to know a man's priorities,

look at:

- how he spends time,
- how he spends money,
- how he handles pressure,
- what he sacrifices for,
- what he refuses to compromise.

Jesus taught,

"For where your treasure is, there will your heart be also."

— Matthew 6:21 (KJV)

Your decisions prove where your heart truly lies.

4. DECISIONS REQUIRE COURAGE, NOT COMFORT

A man must choose the hard thing

when the easy thing tempts him.

Hard decisions:

- saying “no,”
- walking away,
- apologizing,
- setting boundaries,
- stepping into leadership,
- forgiving deeply,
- changing habits,
- choosing righteousness.

Cowards choose what feels good.

Men choose what does good.

Courage is the fuel of righteous decisions.

5. DECISIONS REFLECT WHO YOU FEAR: GOD OR PEOPLE

A man who makes decisions to please people

becomes a slave to opinions.

A man who makes decisions to honor God

becomes a warrior of purpose.

Proverbs 29:25 warns,

"The fear of man bringeth a snare."

Every time you fear people more than God,

you trap yourself.

Fear of God breaks the trap.

Fear of God clarifies decisions.

Fear of God establishes courage.

When a man fears God first,

he decides boldly and cleanly.

6. DECISIONS REQUIRE WISDOM, NOT EMOTION

Emotions are terrible decision-makers.

Wisdom is the reliable guide.

Emotions:

- exaggerate,
- confuse,
- react,
- cloud judgment.

Wisdom:

- clarifies,
- stabilizes,
- reveals truth,
- protects destiny.

Proverbs 19:2 says,

"He that hasteth with his feet sinneth."

Quick decisions made in emotion
produce long-term consequences.

Slow decisions made in wisdom
produce long-term blessings.

7. DECISIONS REQUIRE COUNSEL, NOT ISOLATION

A strong man does not make decisions alone

when wisdom is needed.

Pride isolates men.

Humility seeks counsel.

Proverbs 11:14 teaches,

"In the multitude of counsellors there is safety."

Safe decisions require:

- perspective,
- mentorship,
- spiritual insight,
- accountability.

A man who refuses counsel

chooses destruction.

A man who embraces counsel

chooses elevation.

8. DECISIONS SHAPE RELATIONSHIPS MORE THAN EMOTIONS DO

Every relationship rises or falls

based on decisions made over time.

Relationships require decisions like:

- the decision to communicate truthfully,
- the decision to listen actively,
- the decision to apologize sincerely,
- the decision to forgive fully,
- the decision to pursue peace,
- the decision to stay present,
- the decision to protect the connection.

Love is emotional.

Commitment is decisional.

Homes fall apart not because of one explosion

but because of thousands of small decisions ignored.

Strong relationships are engineered

by strong decisions.

9. DECISIONS DETERMINE SPIRITUAL GROWTH

Spiritual maturity is not automatic.

It is the result of daily decisions.

A man must decide:

- to pray,
- to study Scripture,
- to obey God,
- to repent quickly,
- to deny his flesh,
- to fast,
- to worship,

- to walk in faith.

Jesus said,

"If any man will come after me, let him deny himself..."

— Luke 9:23 (KJV)

Spiritual growth requires decisive discipline.

10. DECISIONS SHAPE DESTINY AND GENERATIONS

Your decisions become your children's reality.

Your decisions shape:

- the emotional climate of your home,
- the opportunities your family receives,
- the confidence your children walk in,
- the future battles they avoid,
- the spiritual foundation they inherit.

Exodus 20:6 promises God's mercy to "thousands"

of generations of those who love Him.

Your decisions today

build momentum for tomorrow.

Your decisions today

echo into eternity.

11. DECISIONS REQUIRE SELF-CONTROL AND DISCIPLINE

A man who cannot discipline himself

cannot trust himself to choose correctly.

Discipline is the muscle of decision-making.

Paul said,

"I therefore so run, not as uncertainly... but I keep under my body..."

— 1 Corinthians 9:26–27 (KJV)

A disciplined man chooses well.

An undisciplined man chooses emotionally.

Consistency produces clarity

and clarity produces better decisions.

12. BAD DECISIONS CAN BE REDEEMED, BUT THEY MUST BE REPLACED BY BETTER DECISIONS

Failure is not final

if decisions change.

Many men repent emotionally

but do not decide practically.

Repentance changes the heart.

Decisions change the direction.

Peter denied Jesus

but made a decision to return.

His future did not depend on his failure

but on his decision after failing.

A man cannot undo the past —

but he can rebuild the future

decision by decision.

13. GREATNESS IS BUILT ON ONE DECISION AT A TIME

The decision:

- to stop making excuses,
- to grow consistently,
- to lead boldly,
- to honor God publicly and privately,
- to stay accountable,
- to master emotions,
- to reject passivity,
- to protect integrity,
- to walk in purpose.

Nothing changes in a man's life

until his decisions change.

Elevation begins with decision.

Healing begins with decision.

Transformation begins with decision.

Destiny begins with decision.

THIS IS THE CALL: MAKE DECISIONS THAT MATCH THE MAN YOU ARE BECOMING

Choose strength.

Choose purpose.

Choose growth.

Choose wisdom.

Choose discipline.

Choose courage.

Choose righteousness.

Choose accountability.

Choose maturity.

Choose destiny.

Choose God.

A man becomes

what he chooses repeatedly.

Because decisions do not just shape days —

they shape destinies.

Decide well.

Decide boldly.

Decide with God.

CHAPTER 12

PURPOSE: THE CALLING THAT DEFINES A MAN

Purpose is the fuel of a man's soul.

It is the invisible calling pulling him forward.

It is the divine assignment written into his very existence.

A man without purpose survives.

A man with purpose **lives**.

A man without purpose wanders.

A man with purpose **walks with intention**.

A man without purpose imitates other men.

A man with purpose becomes the man he was designed to be.

Purpose is not accidental.

Purpose is eternal.

God said to Jeremiah,

"Before I formed thee... I ordained thee."

— Jeremiah 1:5 (KJV)

Before you were born,

before you were named,

before you took your first breath —

purpose was assigned to you.

Your existence is proof

that your assignment is needed.

1. PURPOSE IS THE ANSWER TO "WHY AM I HERE?"

A man who does not know why he exists

will spend his life existing for the wrong reasons.

He will:

- chase money without meaning,

- seek status without substance,
- pursue applause without fulfillment,
- fill time but never fulfill destiny.

Purpose answers the deepest question of a man's heart:

"What was I created to do?"

Proverbs 20:5 says,

"Counsel in the heart of man is like deep water; but a man of understanding will draw it out."

Purpose is deep —

you must draw it out.

2. PURPOSE GIVES A MAN IDENTITY

Identity is not found in:

- job titles,
- physical strength,
- social status,

- financial accomplishments,
- public praise.

Identity is found in **calling**.

A man's identity is strengthened

when his purpose becomes clear.

You are not defined by:

- your mistakes,
- your past,
- your upbringing,
- your failures,
- your weaknesses.

You are defined by the One who created you.

David discovered identity when purpose found him:

"Rise and anoint him: for this is he."

— 1 Samuel 16:12 (KJV)

Purpose tells a man who he is

and what he is not.

3. PURPOSE GIVES A MAN FOCUS

A man without purpose tries to do everything.

A man with purpose does the right things.

Purpose strengthens your "yes"

and protects your "no."

Purpose eliminates:

- distractions,
- confusion,
- emotional impulses,
- wasted years.

Paul said,

"This one thing I do..."

— Philippians 3:13 (KJV)

Purpose simplifies a man's life.

Purpose cuts away what does not matter.

You cannot focus on your assignment

while you're entertaining your distractions.

4. PURPOSE GIVES A MAN STRENGTH IN HARD TIMES

Purpose gives meaning to suffering.

Purpose helps a man say:

"This pain has a purpose."

"This season is preparing me."

"This pressure is shaping me."

"This hardship is developing me."

Romans 8:28 declares,

"All things work together for good..."

Purpose transforms obstacles into opportunities.

Purpose turns pain into preparation.

Purpose turns trials into training.

A man who knows his purpose

cannot be broken easily —

because he understands what is being built.

5. PURPOSE REVEALS WHY CERTAIN BATTLES FIND YOU

Every battle in your life has purpose connected to it.

Some battles come:

- to strengthen you,
- to sharpen you,
- to humble you,
- to awaken you,
- to equip you,
- to prepare you for greater influence.

David fought bears and lions

because purpose required a giant slayer.

Joseph endured betrayal

because purpose required leadership in Egypt.

Jesus endured the cross

because purpose required resurrection.

Purpose explains the battles others do not understand.

6. PURPOSE IS DISCOVERED THROUGH GOD, NOT THE WORLD

Purpose is spiritual.

Purpose is divine.

Purpose comes from the Creator, not the culture.

You cannot find purpose in:

- comparison,
- trends,

- money,
- popularity,
- social media,
- job titles.

Purpose is revealed in the presence of God.

Proverbs 3:5–6 says,

"He shall direct thy paths."

Purpose becomes clear

when God becomes first.

7. PURPOSE IS REVEALED ONE STEP AT A TIME

Purpose unfolds slowly — intentionally.

God does not reveal every detail at once

because purpose requires trust.

Abraham was only given the first instruction:

"Get thee out..."

— Genesis 12:1 (KJV)

He wasn't given the full plan

because purpose is discovered step by step.

Every step of obedience

opens the next step of purpose.

Purpose is not a destination —

it is a journey.

8. PURPOSE REQUIRES PROCESS

Purpose is not microwaved.

Purpose is marinated.

God develops a man before He deploys him.

The process:

- humbles pride,
- builds character,
- strengthens faith,
- refines gifts,
- expands wisdom.

Joseph was processed.

Moses was processed.

David was processed.

Paul was processed.

Process is not punishment —

process is preparation.

Galatians 6:9 promises a "due season"

to those who do not faint.

Your purpose will manifest

in due season.

9. PURPOSE BRINGS PEACE

When a man steps into purpose,

internal chaos decreases.

Peace increases because:

- he knows where he's going,
- he knows who he is,
- he knows what matters,
- he knows what to ignore.

Isaiah 26:3 says,

"Thou wilt keep him in perfect peace, whose mind is stayed on thee."

Purpose-focused men

have peace-focused minds.

10. PURPOSE DIRECTS YOUR WALK WITH GOD

Purpose clarifies your spiritual life:

- what you pray for,
- what you study,
- what you fight against,
- what you fast about,
- what you focus on.

Purpose shapes your devotion.

Your spiritual routines are not random —

they're strategic.

Your warfare is not random —

it's purpose-related.

Your anointing is not random —

it is assignment-based.

Purpose aligns a man with heaven.

11. PURPOSE DEFINES THE SEASONS OF YOUR LIFE

Every season has significance:

The waiting season

— strengthens patience.

The wilderness season

— strengthens faith.

The grinding season

— strengthens discipline.

The preparation season

— strengthens consistency.

The elevation season

— strengthens stewardship.

Purpose turns seasons into strategy.

12. PURPOSE SHAPES HOW YOU CHOOSE FRIENDS

Not everyone is assigned to your purpose.

Some people:

- drain you,
- mislead you,
- distract you,
- slow you,
- tempt you,
- discourage you.

But God sends people who:

- sharpen you,
- strengthen you,
- challenge you,
- push you,

- protect your calling.

Proverbs 27:17 says,

"Iron sharpeneth iron..."

Purpose requires purposeful relationships.

13. PURPOSE REQUIRES COURAGE TO LEAVE COMFORT ZONES

Purpose will always require you to outgrow:

- mindsets,
- habits,
- environments,
- people,
- fears.

Comfort is the killer of purpose.

Growth demands leaving what is easy.

Purpose begins

where comfort ends.

14. PURPOSE BECOMES THE LEGACY YOU LEAVE BEHIND

Purpose outlives you.

It shapes:

- your children's confidence,
- your family's direction,
- your lineage's identity,
- your name's reputation,
- your impact on the world.

Psalm 112:6 says,

"The righteous shall be in everlasting remembrance."

Purpose creates remembrance.

Purpose creates legacy.

Purpose creates generational momentum.

THIS IS THE CALL: STEP INTO THE PURPOSE GOD HAS WRITTEN FOR YOUR LIFE

You were not born to be average.

You were not created to blend in.

You were not called to stay hidden.

You were not designed to live small.

You were created:

- to lead,
- to rise,
- to influence,
- to change things,
- to build,
- to carry light,

- to walk in strength,
- to fulfill destiny.

Purpose is not waiting on God —

God is waiting on you.

Walk boldly.

Walk faithfully.

Walk obediently.

Walk intentionally.

Because purpose is the calling

that defines a man.

CHAPTER 13

LEGACY: WHAT A MAN LEAVES BEHIND

Legacy is not built by chance —

it is built by choice.

Every day a man is writing chapters

his children will one day read.

Every decision you make,

every word you speak,

every act of leadership you demonstrate

becomes part of your family's future narrative.

You are building legacy

whether you realize it or not.

But only intentional men

build godly legacy.

Psalm 112:6 says,

"The righteous shall be in everlasting remembrance."

Remembrance is the fruit of righteousness.

Legacy is the echo of obedience.

1. LEGACY IS A MAN'S FINAL MESSAGE

Even after your voice goes silent,

your life will continue to speak.

Your actions will preach louder than your words.

Your consistency will speak louder than your promises.

Your integrity will speak louder than your resume.

Your discipline will speak louder than your intentions.

Your obedience will speak louder than your gifts.

A man's life delivers a sermon

long after he has left the pulpit of earth.

Hebrews 11:4 says of Abel,

"He being dead yet speaketh."

Legacy is your life still speaking

after you are gone.

2. LEGACY IS BUILT THROUGH DAILY EXAMPLE, NOT OCCASIONAL EXCELLENCE

Children are not shaped by a few "big moments."

They are shaped by daily patterns.

They remember:

- who you were consistently,
- how you lived daily,
- how you treated people regularly,
- how you responded repeatedly.

Legacy is not made through one great act —

it is formed through sustained faithfulness.

Your daily habits

become their permanent memories.

Your daily attitudes

become their emotional blueprint.

Your daily decisions

become their future expectations.

Consistency creates legacy.

Inconsistency weakens it.

3. LEGACY IS THE CULTURE YOU SET INSIDE YOUR HOME

A man sets the temperature of his house.

Your:

- tone,
- leadership,
- habits,

- discipline,
- affection,
- spiritual life,
- emotional balance,
- integrity,
- work ethic,

create the atmosphere your family breathes.

You determine:

- whether your home is peaceful or stressful,
- structured or chaotic,
- spiritually alive or spiritually empty,
- emotionally safe or emotionally fragile.

Your presence shapes the environment.

Your example shapes the expectations.

Your leadership shapes the culture.

Generations will breathe the air

you allow.

4. LEGACY IS THE SPIRITUAL COVERING YOU PROVIDE

A man is not just a leader —

he is a covering.

Your prayers cover your household.

Your authority protects their future.

Your anointing breaks generational patterns.

Your faith strengthens their identity.

Your walk with God opens spiritual doors.

When you kneel in prayer,

your family rises in protection.

Job prayed daily over his children, saying,

"It may be that my sons have sinned..."

— Job 1:5 (KJV)

He interceded for battles

they did not even know they were in.

That is what legacy looks like.

5. LEGACY IS THE HEALING YOU FIGHT FOR

Many men inherited:

- trauma,
- dysfunction,
- abandonment,
- emotional silence,
- anger patterns,
- addictions,
- broken marriages,

- unstable households.

But legacy is not just what you pass forward —

it is what you break.

God can use you to stop:

- generational fear,
- generational fatherlessness,
- generational addiction,
- generational instability,
- generational brokenness.

Your healing becomes their inheritance.

Your emotional growth becomes their protection.

Your discipline becomes their normal.

Your stability becomes their foundation.

If dysfunction ran in your family,

let it run **into you**

and go no further.

6. LEGACY IS BUILT IN HOW YOU LOVE

A man's love echoes for generations.

Your love teaches them:

- how to choose a spouse,
- how to show respect,
- how to handle conflict,
- how to express affection,
- how to build security.

Your children are watching

how you love their mother.

Your marriage becomes their classroom.

Your romantic decisions

become their relationship expectations.

Ephesians 5:25 commands,

"Husbands, love your wives…"

Your love shapes their worldview.

7. LEGACY IS SHOWN IN HOW YOU HANDLE FAILURE

Every man fails —

but how he responds to failure

defines his legacy.

When you fail:

- do you deny it or own it?
- hide or heal?
- collapse or correct?
- replay it or rise from it?

Your children don't need a perfect man —

they need a restored man.

They need a man who repents deeply,

grows honestly,

and rises humbly.

Proverbs 24:16 says,

"A just man falleth seven times, and riseth up again."

Your resilience becomes their template.

8. LEGACY IS THE CHARACTER YOU DEVELOP WHEN NO ONE IS WATCHING

Character is not built in crowds.

It is built:

- in private battles,

- in disciplined decisions,
- in unseen moments,
- in private obedience.

The life you live in the dark

determines the light you leave behind.

Legacy is shaped by who you are

when only God sees.

And Psalm 139:1 reminds us,

"O LORD, thou hast searched me, and known me."

Legacy is a private process

with public results.

9. LEGACY IS THE PURPOSE YOU ACTIVATE

When a man activates his God-given purpose,

he unlocks generational influence.

Purpose creates:

- opportunities for others,
- protection for families,
- inspiration for sons,
- confidence for daughters,
- direction for households.

Your purpose is not just about you —

it is about everyone connected to you.

When David stepped into purpose,

his entire nation was impacted.

Purpose multiplies.

Purpose expands.

Purpose transfers.

Purpose influences.

10. LEGACY IS THE VALUES YOU REFUSE TO Surrender

Every family has values.

Some are inherited.

Some are created.

Some are lost.

Some are revived.

But values must be protected by leadership.

A man of legacy guards:

- faith,
- honor,
- respect,
- truth,
- diligence,
- humility,
- courage,
- discipline.

You are not just raising children —

you are raising future husbands,

future wives,

future mothers,

future fathers,

future leaders.

Values shape generations.

11. LEGACY IS WHAT YOU BUILD THAT OTHERS CAN STAND ON

What you build today

becomes their foundation tomorrow.

Your:

- faith,
- sacrifices,
- decisions,
- corrections,

- battles,
- victories,
- prayers,
- consistency,

become spiritual bricks in their future lives.

Psalm 145:4 says,

"One generation shall praise thy works to another."

Legacy is generational testimony.

12. LEGACY IS THE STORY GOD WRITES THROUGH YOUR OBEDIENCE

Legacy is not just your biography —

it is your testimony.

It is God using your life

to reveal His goodness

to everyone who comes after you.

When you obey:

- God writes His glory into your family,
- your lineage becomes stronger,
- generational blessings appear,
- spiritual doors open,
- divine favor becomes inheritance.

Legacy is heaven continuing your story

after earth buries your body.

THIS IS THE CALL: BE A MAN WHO BUILDS LEGACY ON PURPOSE

Legacy is not accidental.

Legacy is intentional.

Legacy is spiritual.

Legacy is generational.

You build it by:

- leading well,

- loving deeply,
- living faithfully,
- fighting battles,
- walking in purpose,
- honoring God,
- protecting your home,
- healing internally,
- standing firm,
- choosing righteousness.

Your legacy begins today.

Tomorrow is built through today's obedience.

Your legacy is God's gift to future generations —

but it begins with your decision to rise now.

Build intentionally.

Build faithfully.

Build spiritually.

Build with conviction.

Build with God.

Because legacy is not what you leave **to** people —

it is what you leave **in** people.

CHAPTER 14

FAITHFULNESS: THE STRENGTH THAT NEVER QUITS

Faithfulness is the measure of a man's maturity.

Faithfulness is the proof of a man's character.

Faithfulness is the anchor of a man's leadership.

Faithfulness is the quiet strength that shapes the world around him.

Not speed.

Not talent.

Not charisma.

Not visibility.

Not applause.

Faithfulness.

Faithfulness is the strength that never quits.

It is the steady pulse of greatness.

It is the hidden engine behind every strong home.

It is the glue that holds marriages together.

It is the structure that stabilizes children's hearts.

It is the foundation of trust.

It is the backbone of purpose.

It is the evidence of true manhood.

Proverbs 20:6 asks,

"But a faithful man who can find?"

It is a rare question

because faithful men are rare men.

And rare men change generations.

1. FAITHFULNESS IS THE COURAGE TO STAY WHEN OTHERS RUN

A faithful man is not moved by storms.

A faithful man does not run when offended.

A faithful man does not flee when uncomfortable.

A faithful man does not abandon responsibility.

Faithfulness looks like:

- Showing up even when tired
- Standing firm even when pressured
- Leading even when overwhelmed
- Serving even when unseen
- Loving even when wounded
- Praying even when weary
- Believing even when discouraged

Faithfulness is not emotional.

Faithfulness is intentional.

Galatians 6:9 says,

"...for in due season we shall reap, if we faint not."

Your faithfulness determines your harvest.

2. FAITHFULNESS IS PROVEN OVER TIME, NOT IN MOMENTS

Anyone can be faithful briefly.

But legacy requires long obedience.

Faithfulness strengthens through:

- seasons of pressure,
- seasons of loneliness,
- seasons of uncertainty,
- seasons of testing,
- seasons of pruning,
- seasons of spiritual stretching.

Faithfulness is revealed in longevity.

It's not about how passionately you start.

It's about how consistently you continue.

Revelation 2:10 says,

"Be thou faithful unto death..."

Not faithful until tired.

Not faithful until frustrated.

Not faithful until challenged.

Faithful unto **death**.

That is the standard of God.

3. FAITHFULNESS IS THE STEADINESS THAT BUILDS EVERYTHING STRONG

What is strong in your life

is strong because you remained faithful long enough to build it.

Your marriage grows through faithfulness.

Your children flourish through faithfulness.

Your finances stabilize through faithfulness.

Your purpose expands through faithfulness.

Your spiritual life deepens through faithfulness.

Your calling matures through faithfulness.

Your character strengthens through faithfulness.

Nothing strong is built quickly.

Everything strong is built consistently.

Faithfulness is the construction crew of greatness.

4. FAITHFULNESS IS A MAN'S ABILITY TO BE TRUSTED

A faithful man becomes a trustworthy man.

Trust is one of the most valuable gifts a man can earn,

but it cannot be demanded.

It must be demonstrated.

You are trusted when:

- your voice is steady,
- your actions align with your words,
- your presence is dependable,
- your responsibilities are fulfilled,
- your character is consistent.

Trust is not built through perfection —

but through predictable integrity.

Luke 16:10 reminds us,

"He that is faithful in that which is least is faithful also in much."

Faithfulness in small things

proves readiness for large things.

5. FAITHFULNESS IS OBEDIENCE WHEN GOD'S INSTRUCTION MAKES NO SENSE

Sometimes God asks a man to:

- stay,
- wait,
- forgive,
- submit,
- sacrifice,
- serve,
- finish,
- trust.

Even when it feels illogical.

Abraham obeyed without full explanation.

Noah built without evidence.

Joseph endured without answers.

David waited without resentment.

Jesus submitted without reluctance.

Faithfulness is obedience

when understanding is absent.

Hebrews 11:8 says,

"By faith Abraham... obeyed; and he went out, not knowing

whither he went."

Faithfulness does not need details —

just direction.

6. FAITHFULNESS IS ENDURANCE IN SPIRITUAL WARFARE

A man is targeted in battle

because he is trusted with purpose.

The enemy attacks your:

- focus,

- commitment,
- self-control,
- discipline,
- consistency,
- integrity,
- spiritual life.

Why?

Because one faithful man

can shift an entire generation.

Faithfulness in warfare looks like:

- praying when attacked,
- fasting when overwhelmed,
- worshipping when discouraged,
- resisting when tempted,
- standing when shaken.

Ephesians 6:13 says,

"...having done all, to stand."

Faithfulness stands.

7. FAITHFULNESS IS PRIVATE VICTORY BEFORE PUBLIC RESPONSIBILITY

Before God promotes a man publicly,

He tests him privately.

He watches:

- how you think
- how you speak
- how you treat people you don't need
- how you steward opportunities
- how you handle opposition
- how you honor your commitments
- how you carry responsibility
- how you obey Him in secret

Your private discipline

qualifies your public influence.

Your hidden devotion

determines your visible destiny.

Matthew 6:6 promises,

"...thy Father which seeth in secret shall reward thee openly."

Faithfulness is a secret seed

with a public harvest.

8. FAITHFULNESS IS THE HEARTBEAT OF MARRIAGE

A marriage grows where faithfulness is planted.

A faithful man:

- protects trust,
- honors covenant,
- communicates openly,
- serves humbly,

- leads spiritually,
- repents sincerely,
- forgives quickly,
- fights fair,
- refuses to quit.

A woman feels safest

in the presence of a faithful man.

Proverbs 31:11 says,

"The heart of her husband doth safely trust in him..."

Faithfulness creates emotional security.

Security creates intimacy.

Intimacy creates unity.

Unity creates longevity.

9. FAITHFULNESS IS THE EXAMPLE CHILDREN REMEMBER

Children do not remember everything a father says —

but they remember who he consistently was.

A faithful father becomes:

- a stable presence,
- a predictable protector,
- a committed provider,
- a steady leader,
- a spiritual anchor.

Children grow confident

when fathers are consistent.

Psalm 103:13 says,

"Like as a father pitieth his children..."

Your faithfulness becomes their foundation.

10. FAITHFULNESS IS A MAN'S GREATEST SPIRITUAL WEAPON

The enemy can outwit men.

He can deceive men.

He can distract men.

He can tempt men.

But he cannot defeat a man

who simply refuses to quit.

Faithfulness breaks cycles.

Faithfulness weakens hell's influence.

Faithfulness confuses the enemy.

Faithfulness multiplies spiritual authority.

Faithfulness unlocks God's favor.

James 1:12 promises,

"Blessed is the man that endureth temptation..."

Blessing is connected to endurance.

11. FAITHFULNESS IS THE PATHWAY TO PROMOTION

You do not pray your way into elevation.

You do not hope your way into opportunities.

You remain faithful

until God elevates you.

Promotion is the fruit of faithfulness.

Joseph was faithful in the pit.

Faithful in the prison.

Faithful in waiting.

Faithful in obedience.

And God placed him in the palace.

Psalm 75:6–7 declares,

"...God is the judge: he putteth down one, and setteth up another."

God promotes faithful men.

12. FAITHFULNESS IS THE FINAL MEASURE OF A MAN

At the end of a man's life,

God will not ask:

- "Were you famous?"
- "Were you impressive?"
- "Were you wealthy?"
- "Were you popular?"
- "Were you talented?"

He will ask one question:

"Were you faithful?"

Matthew 25:21 records heaven's highest commendation:

"Well done, thou good and faithful servant…"

God celebrates faithfulness

above everything else.

THIS IS THE CALL: BE THE MAN WHO NEVER QUITS

Stand when weak.

Show up when tired.

Lead when afraid.

Stay when pressured.

Serve when unseen.

Worship when wounded.

Pray when discouraged.

Finish what you start.

Keep your word.

Guard your integrity.

Stay committed.

Honor God.

Hold the line.

Endure the storm.

Rise again.

Remain faithful.

Because faithfulness

is the strength

that builds great men,

strengthens great homes,

sustains great marriages,

develops great leaders,

and earns heaven's reward.

Be the man who stays.

Be the man who endures.

Be the man who finishes.

Be the man God calls **faithful**.

CHAPTER 15

THE STAND: WHEN A MAN RISES INTO GOD'S DESIGN

There is a moment in every man's journey

when he feels the unmistakable pull of destiny.

It is not loud,

not dramatic,

not always convenient,

but it is undeniable.

It is the moment when God whispers,

"Rise."

It is the moment when a man must decide

whether he will continue living in who he has been

or step into who he was created to be.

The distance between a man's potential

and a man's purpose

is bridged by one decision:

The Stand.

Ephesians 6:13 commands,

"...and having done all, to stand."

Standing is not physical posture —

it is spiritual position.

It is the alignment of a man's will with God's calling.

1. A MAN'S STAND IS THE MOMENT HE REFUSES TO LIVE SMALL

Before a man can rise,

he must first refuse to shrink.

He refuses:

- small thinking,

- small living,
- small vision,
- small discipline,
- small expectations,
- small faith.

A man stands when he declares:

"I was made for more than survival."

"I was created for more than cycles."

"I am destined for more than excuses."

"I am called to live fully — not quietly."

Isaiah 60:1 calls to the man inside you:

"Arise, shine; for thy light is come..."

You cannot shine

until you stand.

2. WHEN A MAN STANDS, HE BREAKS AGREEMENT WITH FEAR

Fear does not govern a standing man.

Before a man stands physically,

he must stand internally.

He must stand against:

- the fear of failure,
- the fear of being inadequate,
- the fear of responsibility,
- the fear of leading,
- the fear of spiritual assignment,
- the fear of becoming what God sees.

2 Timothy 1:7 declares,

"For God hath not given us the spirit of fear..."

Standing is the refusal

to negotiate with fear any longer.

3. WHEN A MAN STANDS, HE ENDS THE REIGN OF EXCUSES

Excuses are the quiet assassins of destiny.

Excuses disguise themselves as reasons.

Excuses present themselves as emotional protection.

Excuses pretend to protect a man's image

while destroying his potential.

But a standing man says:

"No more excuses."

"No more blaming my past."

"No more blaming others."

"No more hiding behind disappointment."

"No more shrinking behind trauma."

"No more delaying obedience."

Standing is the death of excuses

and the birth of transformation.

4. WHEN A MAN STANDS, THE ATMOSPHERE OF HIS HOME CHANGES

A man's stand is not personal —

it is generational.

When a man stands:

- anxiety decreases,
- stability increases,
- clarity rises,
- trust grows,
- hope returns,
- unity strengthens,
- God's order reestablishes itself.

Your stand sets the emotional, spiritual, and structural tone of your home.

Joshua's declaration

was not a suggestion,

not a philosophy,

not a theory.

It was a stand:

"...as for me and my house, we will serve the LORD."

— Joshua 24:15 (KJV)

Your stand becomes your home's covering.

]

5. WHEN A MAN STANDS, CHILDREN GAIN CONFIDENCE

Children look for heroes —

but they don't need fictional ones.

They need a father who stands.

A standing father creates:

- security,
- identity,

- boldness,
- emotional grounding,
- spiritual direction,
- generational strength.

When children feel the presence of a standing father, they breathe easier.

Psalm 112:2 says,

"His seed shall be mighty upon earth..."

Your stand becomes their strength.

6. WHEN A MAN STANDS, HE STEPS OUT OF HIS OLD SELF

A man cannot stand and stay the same.

Standing is shedding:

- old habits,
- old anger,

- old insecurities,
- old patterns,
- old emotional wounds,
- old ways of thinking.

Standing requires death to the former man

and birth of the new one.

Ephesians 4:24 commands,

"Put on the new man..."

Standing is spiritual clothing —

you put on who you were always meant to be.

7. WHEN A MAN STANDS IN GOD, HE CONFUSES THE ENEMY

The enemy expects weakness.

He expects wavering.

He expects inconsistency.

But when a man stands:

- temptation loses power,
- distractions lose influence,
- spiritual attacks lose momentum,
- cycles lose repetition,
- hell loses access.

Standing is warfare.

Standing is resistance.

Standing is victory in slow motion.

James 4:7 says,

"Resist the devil, and he will flee..."

Resisting is standing.

8. WHEN A MAN STANDS, HE BECOMES A BUILDER

A standing man does not merely survive —

he builds.

He builds:

- faith,
- discipline,
- structure,
- vision,
- purpose,
- spiritual infrastructure,
- emotional balance,
- relational strength.

A standing man looks at broken pieces

and starts rebuilding with conviction.

Nehemiah rebuilt Jerusalem

not because he had skill

but because he had **stand**.

9. WHEN A MAN STANDS, HE BECOMES THE LEADER HIS FAMILY NEEDS

Leadership is not loud —

it is consistent.

Leadership is not forceful —

it is faithful.

Leadership is not domination —

it is direction.

Leadership is not control —

it is conviction.

A standing man:

- leads by example,

- leads by discipline,
- leads by spiritual maturity,
- leads by kindness,
- leads by accountability,
- leads by vision,
- leads by humility,
- leads by obedience.

Proverbs 29:18 says,

"Where there is no vision, the people perish..."

Your stand becomes their vision.

10. WHEN A MAN STANDS, HE ACTIVATES HEAVEN'S BACKING

Standing is not just natural —

it is supernatural.

When you stand:

- angels are assigned,
- favor is released,
- strength is imparted,
- wisdom is granted,
- clarity is given,
- doors open,
- strongholds break.

God does not empower sitting men —

He empowers standing men.

1 Corinthians 16:13 commands,

"Watch ye, stand fast in the faith, quit you like men, be strong."

Heaven respects a man who stands.

11. WHEN A MAN STANDS, HE MAKES A DECISION THE FUTURE WILL THANK HIM FOR

Some decisions you make are not for today.

They are for:

- your future self,
- your future marriage,
- your future children,
- your future grandchildren.

A man's stand echoes into generations.

Psalm 145:4 says,

"One generation shall praise thy works to another..."

Your stand becomes their testimony.

12. THE FINAL CALL: TAKE YOUR STAND NOW

Standing is not a feeling.

Standing is not a mood.

Standing is not a phase.

Standing is a **decision**.

A decision to:

- rise,
- grow,
- mature,
- lead,
- build,
- repent,
- strengthen,
- submit to God,
- protect,
- obey,

- endure,
- overcome.

A decision to stop retreating.

A decision to stop shrinking.

A decision to stop apologizing for your calling.

A decision to stop running from responsibility.

A decision to stop living beneath your anointing.

A decision to finally become

the man God designed all along.

Heaven does not ask for perfection —

it asks for your stand.

Ephesians 6:13 closes the instruction with clarity:

"...and having done all, to stand."

This is the moment.

This is the call.

This is the rise.

Stand with courage.

Stand with conviction.

Stand with strength.

Stand with unwavering faith.

Stand in the authority of God.

Stand in the boldness of identity.

Stand in the power of purpose.

Because when a man stands —

everything connected to him

rises.

REFLECTION PAGES

REFLECT. RESET. RISE.

These reflection pages are designed to help you internalize the journey you've taken through this book.
This is your moment to pause, examine, and align your heart with the man you are becoming — the man God designed you to be.

Take your time.
Write honestly.
Reflect deeply.
Rise intentionally.

Reflection 1

Who Am I Becoming?

"Examine me, O LORD, and prove me; try my reins and my heart."
— Psalm 26:2 (KJV)

Guiding Thought:

The strongest men are those who examine themselves before God does.
Who you are becoming matters more than who you've been.

Reflection Space:

- What patterns in my life need to change?
- What strengths do I need to develop?
- What version of myself am I stepping into as I lead well?

Write your reflections below:

WHEN MEN LEAD WELL

Reflection 2

My Stand

"...and having done all, to stand."

— Ephesians 6:13 (KJV)

Guiding Thought:

Every man reaches a defining moment when he decides to stand — for truth, for family, for purpose, for God.

Reflection Space:

- What does "standing" mean for me in this season?
- Where have I been wavering?
- Where must I stand more firmly?

Write your reflections below:

WHEN MEN LEAD WELL

Reflection 3

Faithfulness in My Daily Life

"A faithful man shall abound with blessings..."

— Proverbs 28:20 (KJV)

Guiding Thought:

Faithfulness is not a concept — it is a lifestyle.

Small acts of consistency form the foundation of great men.

Reflection Space:

- Where am I being faithful?
- Where has inconsistency weakened me?
- What new habits must I build to lead well?

Write your reflections below:

WHEN MEN LEAD WELL

Reflection 4 — My Legacy Begins Now

"A good man leaveth an inheritance to his children's children..."
— Proverbs 13:22 (KJV)

Guiding Thought:
Legacy is not something you leave when you die — it's something you live while you're alive.

Reflection Space:

- What kind of legacy am I building with my choices today?
- What do I want my children or future generations to say about me?
- What must I start — and what must I stop — to build that legacy?

Write your reflections below:

WHEN MEN LEAD WELL

Reflection 5

The Man God Sees in Me

"Before I formed thee... I ordained thee."
— Jeremiah 1:5 (KJV)

Guiding Thought:
God's design for you is greater than your doubts about yourself.
Your purpose existed before your insecurities did.

Reflection Space:

- What has God spoken about me that I have ignored or doubted?
- Where is God calling me higher?
- What fears do I need to surrender to walk in His design?

Write your reflections below:

Reflection 6

What I Must Protect

"Keep thy heart with all diligence; for out of it are the issues of life."

— Proverbs 4:23 (KJV)

Guiding Thought:

A man's strength is not only in what he builds — but in what he protects.

Reflection Space:

- What mindsets, relationships, and habits must I guard?
- What influences must I remove from my life?
- Where is the enemy trying to weaken my foundation?

Write your reflections below:

Reflection 7

My Next Step Forward

"The steps of a good man are ordered by the LORD..."

— Psalm 37:23 (KJV)

Guiding Thought:

Growth is intentional.

God orders your steps, but you must decide to take them.

Reflection Space:

- What is the first step I must take after finishing this book?
- What accountability do I need?
- What commitment am I ready to make?

Write your reflections below:

WHEN MEN LEAD WELL

ADDITIONAL SCRIPTURES FOR REFLECTION PAGES

STRENGTH & COURAGE

Joshua 1:9

"Be strong and of a good courage; be not afraid... for the LORD thy God is with thee whithersoever thou goest." **(KJV)**

Psalm 27:1

"The LORD is my light and my salvation; whom shall I fear?..." **(KJV)**

1 Corinthians 16:13

"Watch ye, stand fast in the faith, quit you like men, be strong." **(KJV)**

Psalm 18:32

"It is God that girdeth me with strength, and maketh my way perfect." **(KJV)**

LEADERSHIP & PURPOSE

Proverbs 16:9

"A man's heart deviseth his way: but the LORD directeth his steps." **(KJV)**

Ephesians 2:10

"For we are his workmanship, created in Christ Jesus unto good works..." **(KJV)**

Proverbs 3:5–6

"In all thy ways acknowledge him, and he shall direct thy paths." **(KJV)**

Isaiah 58:11

"And the LORD shall guide thee continually..." **(KJV)**

LEGACY & GENERATIONAL IMPACT

Psalm 112:1–2

"Blessed is the man that feareth the LORD... His seed shall be mighty upon earth." **(KJV)**

Deuteronomy 7:9

"...the LORD thy God... keepeth covenant and mercy... to a thousand generations." **(KJV)**

Psalm 78:6

"That the generation to come might know them..." **(KJV)**

Proverbs 20:7

"The just man walketh in his integrity: his children are blessed after him." **(KJV)**

DISCIPLINE & CHARACTER

Hebrews 12:11

"Now no chastening for the present seemeth to be joyous... but afterward it yieldeth the peaceable fruit of righteousness..." **(KJV)**

Proverbs 25:28

"He that hath no rule over his own spirit is like a city... without walls." **(KJV)**

Psalm 119:133

"Order my steps in thy word: and let not any iniquity have dominion over me." **(KJV)**

1 Peter 5:6

"Humble yourselves therefore under the mighty hand of God, that he may exalt you in due time." **(KJV)**

FAITHFULNESS & ENDURANCE

James 1:12

"Blessed is the man that endureth temptation..." **(KJV)**

Galatians 6:9

"...for in due season we shall reap, if we faint not." **(KJV)**

Revelation 2:10

"Be thou faithful unto death, and I will give thee a crown of life." **(KJV)**

Psalm 31:24

"Be of good courage, and he shall strengthen your heart..." **(KJV)**

SPIRITUAL WARFARE & STANDING

Isaiah 54:17

"No weapon that is formed against thee shall prosper..." **(KJV)**

James 4:7

"Resist the devil, and he will flee from you." **(KJV)**

Psalm 144:1

"Blessed be the LORD my strength, which teacheth my hands to war..." **(KJV)**

Ephesians 6:10–11

"Finally, my brethren, be strong in the Lord... Put on the whole armour of God..." **(KJV)**

IDENTITY, HONOR & MANHOOD

Micah 6:8

"...to do justly, and to love mercy, and to walk humbly with thy God?" **(KJV)**

Psalm 1:1–3

"...his delight is in the law of the LORD... and he shall be like a tree planted..." **(KJV)**

Proverbs 4:7

"Wisdom is the principal thing; therefore get wisdom..." **(KJV)**

Psalm 15:1–2

"He that walketh uprightly, and worketh righteousness..." **(KJV)**

BROKENNESS, HEALING & TRANSFORMATION

Psalm 34:18

"The LORD is nigh unto them that are of a broken heart..." **(KJV)**

Ezekiel 36:26

"A new heart also will I give you, and a new spirit will I put within you..." **(KJV)**

Isaiah 43:19

"Behold, I will do a new thing..." **(KJV)**

Philippians 1:6

"...he which hath begun a good work in you will perform it..." **(KJV)**

FAITH, OBEDIENCE & WALKING WITH GOD

Hebrews 11:6

"But without faith it is impossible to please him..." **(KJV)**

Psalm 37:23–24

"Though he fall, he shall not be utterly cast down..." **(KJV)**

Romans 8:37

"...we are more than conquerors through him that loved us." **(KJV)**

Deuteronomy 31:6

"Be strong and of a good courage... he will not fail thee, nor forsake thee." **(KJV)**

FINAL PRAYER

A Prayer for the Man I Am Becoming

Heavenly Father,

I come before You as a man who desires to grow,

to rise,

to lead well,

to walk in purpose,

and to honor You with my life.

Lord, strengthen me where I am weak.

Build me where I am broken.

Correct me where I am misaligned.

Restore me where I have fallen short.

Shape me into the man You designed

before the foundations of the world.

Give me the courage to stand with conviction,
the discipline to walk in righteousness,
the endurance to remain faithful,
and the wisdom to lead those You've entrusted to me.

Teach me to love with patience,
to serve with humility,
to act with integrity,
and to lead with compassion.

Help me to break cycles that have traveled through generations
and establish a legacy of strength, honor, faith, and obedience.

Let my life be an example to my children,
a blessing to my home,
a pillar for my community,
and a testimony of Your grace.

Lord, order my steps according to Your Word.

Guard my heart.

Renew my mind.

Strengthen my spirit.

Empower my hands to build what You have called me to build.

Remove every distraction,

silence every lie,

close every wrong door,

and illuminate the right path.

Make me a man who stands

when others fall back,

who speaks truth with love,

who lives with purpose,

and who leads with honor.

And Father,

may everything I do reflect Your glory.

May my decisions point to Your wisdom.

May my legacy reveal Your faithfulness.

May my life bear fruit that remains.

Thank You for calling me.

Thank You for shaping me.

Thank You for strengthening me.

Thank You for trusting me to lead well.

I commit myself—heart, mind, soul, and strength—

to becoming the man You intended,

the leader my family needs,

and the example future generations will thank You for.

In Jesus' mighty name,

Amen.

ABOUT THE AUTHOR

Lemuel King is an author, speaker, and leadership voice committed to restoring purpose, responsibility, and integrity in men, families, and communities. Through his writing, he challenges men to move beyond passive influence and step fully into leadership that is intentional, accountable, and rooted in faith.

Drawing from real-life experience in education, mentorship, ministry, and community engagement, Lemuel King writes with clarity, conviction, and compassion. His work consistently addresses the practical realities men face—decision-making, discipline, identity, pressure, and legacy—while calling them to lead well in their homes, workplaces, and spheres of influence.

When Men Lead Well continues his mission of equipping men to understand that leadership is not about position, control, or recognition, but about responsibility, consistency, and character. Lemuel King believes that when men lead with wisdom and humility, environments shift, families strengthen, and future generations benefit.

Lemuel King is affiliated with **KTURN**, a leadership and motivational platform centered on the principle of *"Making a Turn for the Better."* Through books, workshops, conferences, and leadership development initiatives, this work supports men, leaders, and communities seeking growth, alignment, and transformation.

For speaking engagements, conferences, workshops, or leadership development opportunities, contact **admin1@mykturn.com**

JOIN THE KTURN MOVEMENT

Making a Turn for the Better

The journey of becoming a stronger man does not end with the final page of this book.

Growth is a daily commitment.

Leadership is a daily choice.

And becoming the man God designed you to be is a daily walk.

That's why KTURN exists.

KTURN is more than a brand—

it is a movement dedicated to Motivation, Inspiration, Encouragement, and Empowerment.

Through books, journals, digital tools, courses, and the upcoming **MIEE App**, we equip men, women, educators, leaders, and families to rise higher and live with purpose.

You are invited to become part of a community committed to growth, faith, and excellence.

Whether you want to build stronger habits, deepen your spiritual walk, or walk boldly in your God-given identity, KTURN has resources designed to strengthen your journey.

CONNECT WITH KTURN

Website:

www.mykturn.com

Email:

admin1@mykturn.com

WHAT'S NEXT FROM KTURN?

✔ Inspirational Books

✔ Journals for Personal Growth

✔ Leadership Development Tools

✔ Faith-Based Resources

✔ The MIEE App (Coming Soon)

✔ Digital Courses & Audio Devotionals

✔ Community Challenges

This is your moment.

Your turning point.

Your invitation to rise.

KTURN is here to walk with you—

step by step,

decision by decision,

chapter by chapter,

as you continue leading well and living well.

www.ingramcontent.com/pod-product-compliance
Lightning Source LLC
LaVergne TN
LVHW010538160826
845677LV00013B/2923